Vedic Mathematics

PRADEEP KUMAR

SHREE Book Centre

SHREE Book Centre
98/B, Dalmia Bldg, Opp Sandesh Hotel,
T.H. Kataria Marg, Matunga (W), Mumbai-400 016 (INDIA)
Tel: 4377516, 4374559 Fax: 4309183
Email: shreebk@vsnl.com

Vedic Mathematics
©2002, Sterling Publishers Private Limited
ISBN 81 796 3019 6

Published by Sterling Publishers Pvt. Ltd., New Delhi-110020.
Lasertypeset by Vikas Compographics, New Delhi-110020.
Printed at : De Unique, New Delhi

PREFACE

All you wanted to know about 'Vedic Mathematics' is a manifestation and a coagulation of genuine illustrations and methods of fast calculations. This magical tool is unique in its field and will serve two purposes:

- It will help enhance the calculating speed of students; and

- Will be beneficial in preparations for the MBA/CAT entrance examinations.

How to use this book

First of all learn all the multiplication methods and techniques explained in this book in the section on multiplication. Do the exercises provided at the end of every topic so that the techniques can be understood completely. Then understand Squaring and Cubing techniques.

After this, whenever you come across a multiplication sum, try to solve that by the formulae and techniques explained in this book. A mere reading of the book from one end to the other will not help in the long run. If you wish to benefit fully, make it a habit to use these methods.

Once you have mastered Multiplication techniques, then you can proceed to the chapters on Division, Square Roots and Cube Roots.

Caution

Do not proceed to the chapter on Square Roots without understanding the chapter on Division completely. They are linked. Understanding the process of square roots without understanding division will be a futile exercise.

After understanding the process of division, and that of square roots and cube roots, make it a habit to use these methods. Simultaneous equations can be learned any time.

CONTENTS

Dedicated to my grandfather,

Late Hazari Prasad Singh,

who always encouraged me to excel

MULTIPLICATION

Multiplication is supposed to be the toughest of all four mathematical operations. Students feel threatened by multiplication.

In this book, I have dealt with this topic in detail.

To make this topic easily graspable, I have divided it into several parts. Each part is full of examples, and steps are explained clearly wherever required. If this helps students, I will feel rewarded.

1. First Formula

I have called this 'First Formula' because in my opinion a person willing to learn 'magical methods of fast calculations' should start from here. The formula will be explained with various examples.

Multiplying two-digit numbers by two-digit numbers

Let us start with an example:

$$\begin{array}{r} 65 \\ \times\,65 \\ \hline \\ \hline \end{array}$$

How would you multiply this in the conventional way? Let us solve it:

$$
\begin{array}{r}
65 \\
\times\ 65 \\
\hline
325 \\
390 \\
\hline
4225 \\
\hline
\end{array}
$$

What are the steps you took here?

- First you multiplied 65 by 5 and wrote it below the line (325).

- Then you multiplied 65 by 6 and wrote it below the first row leaving one space from the right (390).

- You added the numbers in the first row with the numbers in the second row by first bringing down the digit on the extreme right and adding the other digits, thereafter, conventionally.

- You got 4225 as the answer.

Now let us do it using the magical method:

$$
\begin{array}{r}
65 \\
\times\ 65 \\
\hline
4225 \\
\hline
\end{array}
$$

What did we do here?

- We multiplied 5 by 5 and put 25 as the right-hand side of the answer.

- We added 1 to the top left digit 6 to make it 7.

- We then multiplied it (7) by the bottom left digit 6 and got 42, which is the left-hand side of the answer.

- We got the correct answer 4225.

Did you get it?

Let us do some more by the method learned just now !

$$\begin{array}{r} 75 \\ \times\ 75 \\ \hline 5625 \\ \hline \end{array}$$

Let me explain the method again !!

- We multiplied 5 by 5 and put 25 on the right-hand side.

- We added 1 to the top left digit 7 to make it 8.

- We then multiplied 8 by the bottom left digit 7 and kept 56 on the left-hand side.

- We arrived at the right answer 5625.

Now the method should be crystal clear to you

In the same manner we can multiply the following:

15 by 15, 25 by 25, 35 by 35, 45 by 45, 55 by 55, etc.

I understand, you are getting inquisitive now and are planning to ask a loaded question.

Your question is whether the applicability of the formula is limited to a number ending with 5 only?

My answer is no, it is not like that.

Let us expand the formula...................

We can apply this formula to multiply a good number of two-digit and three-digit numbers.

Pre-condition

Left-hand digits should be the same and the total of right-hand digits should be 10.

Let us take an example:

$$
\begin{array}{r}
66 \\
\times\ 64 \\
\hline
4224 \\
\end{array}
$$

In this example the left-hand digits are the same - i.e. 6, and the total of the right-hand digits is 10. So we can apply this formula here.

Can we apply the same formula to the following?

(1)	67	(2)	68	(3)	69
	× 63		× 62		× 61
	4221		4216		4209

Yes, we can apply the same formula to all these since their left-hand digits are the same and the total of the right-hand digits is 10.

Here, another question may creep into your mind that in the third example above, when 9 is multiplied by 1, the answer is 9, Then why do we put 09 there. The answer is simple. From all the above examples we have learned that the right-hand side should have two digits. But we are getting only one digit, i.e. 9. So what do we do? How can we use this without changing its value? Just add a 0 to the left. Now see whether your formula is applicable to the following examples:

(1)	46	**(2)**	47
	× 44		× 43

(3)	48	**(4)**	49
	× 42		× 41

I know that your answer is affirmative and you can write the answers as 2024, 2021, 2016 and 2009.

Problems:

Apply your formula to the following and write the answers.

(1)	81	**(2)**	97	**(3)**	87
	× 89		× 93		× 83

(4)	58	**(5)**	36	**(6)**	53
	× 52		× 34		× 57

(7)	22	(8)	78	(9)	39
	× 28		× 72		× 31

Answers:

1. 7209
2. 9021
3. 7221
4. 3016
5. 1224
6. 3021
7. 616
8. 5616
9. 1209

Multiplying three-digit numbers by three-digit numbers.

Having done this for the two-digit numbers, can we extend the same formula to the three-digit numbers? The answer is yes, we can do that.

> In the case of three-digit numbers the first two-digits on the left should be the same and the total of the digits on the right should be 10.

Let us take an example:

$$\begin{array}{r} 115 \\ \times\,115 \\ \hline \\ \hline \end{array}$$

In the case mentioned above, the first two-digits on the left-hand side are the same (11) and the total of the right-hand digits is 10, so we can apply our formula here.

The steps will be:

- Multiply 5 by 5 and keep 25 on the right-hand side.
- Add 1 to 11 to make it 12.
- Multiply 12 by 11 and put 132 on the left-hand side. Our operation is complete.
- The answer is 13225.

You can apply this technique to these sums also:

(1)
$$\begin{array}{r} 116 \\ \times\,114 \\ \hline \end{array}$$

(2)
$$\begin{array}{r} 117 \\ \times\,113 \\ \hline \end{array}$$

(3)
$$\begin{array}{r} 118 \\ \times\,112 \\ \hline \end{array}$$

(4)
$$\begin{array}{r} 119 \\ \times\,111 \\ \hline \end{array}$$

Answers:

1. 13224   **2.** 13221   **3.** 13216   **4.** 13209

Problems:

(1)	125 × 125	**(2)**	126 × 124
(3)	137 × 133	**(4)**	139 × 131
(5)	146 × 144	**(6)**	148 × 142
(7)	169 × 161	**(8)**	164 × 166
(9)	153 × 157	**(10)**	158 × 152

Answers:

1. 15625   **2.** 15624   **3.** 18221   **4.** 18209

5. 21024   **6.** 21016   **7.** 27209   **8.** 27224

9. 24021   **10.** 24016

Applications:

The utility of First Formula is very wide. You can use this formula to multiply two-digit numbers when the first digits are the same, but the total of the last digits does not come to ten. Say 67 × 65. What will you do in this case?

67 × 65 can be written as (65 + 2) × 65
From our First Formula we know that
65 × 65 = 4225.

Further we are required to add 2 × 65 = 130 to 4225.

The answer is 4355.

$$67 \times 65 = (65 + 2) \times 65$$

$$
\begin{array}{r}
65 \\
\times\, 65 \\
\hline
+\, 2 \times 65 \\
4225 \\
\hline
4225 + \quad 130 \\
\hline
4355
\end{array}
$$

Can you apply the technique used above to find out what 68 × 64 equals to.

Let us see how:
You can break down 68 × 64 in two ways.

Let us solve these:

1. 68 × (62 + 2) and
   (66 + 2) × 64

Let us solve these:

1. $68 \times (62 + 2) = 68 \times 62 + 68 \times 2$
$= 4216 + 136$
$= 4352$

2. $(66 + 2) \times 64 = 66 \times 64 + 2 \times 64$
$= 4224 + 128$
$= 4352$

In the way mentioned above, you can multiply a whole range of numbers. Let us take some more examples to clarify.

Examples:

1. $77 \times 76 = $ (a) $77 \times (73 + 3) = 5621 + 231 = 5852$
$= $ (b) $(74 + 3) \times 76 = 5624 + 228 = 5852$

2. $78 \times 76 = $ (a) $78 \times (72 + 4) = 5616 + 312 = 5928$
$= $ (b) $(74 + 4) \times 76 = 5624 + 304 = 5928$

3. $119 \times 114 = $ (a) $119 \times (111 + 3) = 13209 + 357 = 13566$
$= $ (b) $(116 + 3) \times 114 = 13224 + 342 = 13566$

Upto this point we have worked with those numbers whose first digits were the same and the total of the last digits exceeded 10. Now let us solve some of the examples where the first digit remains the same but the total of the last digits is less than 10.

<u>Let me take an example:</u>

47×42

In this case our first digits are the same (4) but the total of the last two digits is less than 10.

$47 \times 42 = 47 \times (43 - 1) = 2021 - 47 = 1974.$

Let us take a few more examples.

Examples:

1. 48×41 = (a) $48 \times (42-1)$ = $2016-48$ = 1968
         = (b) $(49-1) \times 41$ = $2009-41$ = 1968

2. 56×53 = (a) $56 \times (54-1)$ = $3024-56$ = 2968
         = (b) $(57-1) \times 53$ = $3021-53$ = 2968

3. 55×54 = (a) $55 \times (55-1)$ = $3025-55$ = 2970
         = (b) $(56-1) \times 54$ = $3024-54$ = 2970

4. 55×53 = (a) $55 \times (55-2)$ = $3025-110$ = 2915
         = (b) $(57-2) \times 53$ = $3021-106$ = 2915

5. 65×62 = (a) $65 \times (65-3)$ = $4225-195$ = 4030
         = (b) $(68-3) \times 62$ = $4216-186$ = 4030

Problems:

(1) 117×112	**(2)** 108×106	**(3)** 124×126
(4) 128×125	**(5)** 122×129	**(6)** 126×129
(7) 128×124	**(8)** 138×133	**(9)** 146×147
(10) 143×148	**(11)** 138×134	**(12)** 117×115

Answers:

1. 13104	**2.** 11448	**3.** 15624
4. 16000	**5.** 15738	**6.** 16254
7. 15872	**8.** 18354	**9.** 21462
10. 21164	**11.** 18492	**12.** 13455

2. Quick Formula

After learning First Formula one should try and learn Quick Formula. This formula is based upon 'Nikhilam' of 'Vedic Mathematics'. I have tried to explain the technique through various examples.

Multiplication of digits near 100

Let me give you a formula for multiplication of digits near 100.

As the name suggests, the base for all our operation will be 100.

Let us start with an example:

$$\begin{array}{r} 87 \\ \times\,89 \\ \hline \\ \hline \end{array}$$

To solve this, we measure the distance of 87 and 89 from 100 and write it in the following manner:

$$\begin{array}{rcl} 87 \;/ & - & 13 \\ \times\,89 \;/ & - & 11 \\ \hline 76 \;/ & & {}_1 43 \quad = \quad 7743 \\ \hline \end{array}$$

Steps explained:

- Our base is 100.

- 87 is 13 less than 100; therefore it is written as 87/ − 13.

- 89 is 11 less than 100; therefore it is written as 89 / − 11.

20

4. Crosswise operation (87–11) or (89–13) gives the same result 76, which we tentatively put as the left part of the answer.

5. For the right part we multiply (–13) and (–11) and get (+ 143), but we can keep only two digits on the right, as our base is 100. Excess digits will be added to the left-hand side. The number of digits on the right-hand side of the slash will be equal to the number of zeros in the base.

6. We get 76 / 143; 1 goes to the left to make it 7743.

7. In other words, we can understand this as:

$$76 / 143$$
$$= 76 \times \text{Base (100)} + 143$$
$$= 7600 + 143$$

Let us look at some more examples.

Examples:

1.
$$\begin{array}{r} 82 \\ \times\ 78 \\ \hline \\ \hline \end{array}$$

This can be written as:

$$\begin{array}{lllll} 82 & / & - & 18 \\ 78 & / & - & 22 \\ \hline \end{array}$$

Operating crosswise, we tentatively get the right part of the answer = 60.

(82–22) or (78 –18) = 60

$$\frac{82\ /-18}{78\ /-22}$$

60 /

Multiplying (–18) and (–22) we get 396.

$$82/-18$$
$$78/-22$$
$$60 / 396 = 6396$$

$$60 \times (Base)\ 100 + 396$$
$$6000 + 396 = 6396$$

2.   87
        $\times\,112$

This can be written as:

$$87\ /\ -\quad 13$$
$$112\ /\ +\quad 12$$

Crosswise operation gives us:

(87 + 12) or (112 -13) = 99

$$87/\ -\ 13$$
$$112/\ +\ 12$$
$$\overline{99/}$$

Multiplying (1-13) and (+12) we get –156.

$$87/\ -\quad 13$$
$$112/\ +\quad 12$$
$$\overline{99/\ -\ 156}$$

99×100 (Base) $- 156 = 9900 - 156 = 9744$

22

3.
$$113$$
$$\times 108$$

$$113 / + 13$$
$$108 / + \quad 8$$

Crosswise operation gives us:

$(113 + 8)$ or $(108 + 13) = 121$

$$113 / + 13$$
$$108 / + \quad 8$$
$$121 /$$

Multiplying $(+13)$ and $(+8)$ we get 104.

$$113 / + 13$$
$$108 / + \quad 8$$
$$121 \ / \ 104$$

121×100 (Base) $+ 104 = 12204$

Problems:

(1)
$$89$$
$$\times 92$$

(2)
$$99$$
$$\times 93$$

(3)
$$98$$
$$\times 84$$

(4)
$$87$$
$$\times 76$$

(5)
$$112$$
$$\times 86$$

(6)
$$108$$
$$\times 89$$

(7)
$$102$$
$$\times 106$$

(8)
$$108$$
$$\times 117$$

(9)
$$116$$
$$\times 94$$

	(10)	83 × 94	(11)	107 × 94	(12)	113 × 102

Answers:

1.	8188	**2.**	9207	**3.**	8232
4.	6612	**5.**	9632	**6.**	9612
7.	10812	**8.**	12636	**9.**	10904
10.	7802	**11.**	10058	**12.**	11526

Multiplication of digits near 50

We have learnt to multiply digits near 100. Now we will learn to multiply digits near 50.

All the operations remain the same; only one thing will change.

Earlier we were operating in the 100 zone, now we will operate in the 100 divided by 2 zone. Therefore we will divide the number obtained after crosswise operation by 2.

Difference of the digits taken from $\frac{100}{2} = 50$

Examples:

1.
$$\begin{array}{r} 62 \\ \times\ 63 \\ \hline \end{array}$$

62 /	+	12
63 /	+	13
75 /		156

> Crosswise operation (62 + 13) or (63 + 12) gives us 75.

$$\frac{75 \times 100\ (\text{Base}}{2} + 156$$

$$3750 + 156 = 3906$$

2.
$$\begin{array}{r} 47 \\ \times\ 64 \\ \hline \end{array}$$

47 /	−	3
64 /	+	14
61 /	−	42

> Crosswise operation (47 + 14) or (64 − 3) gives us 61.

$$\frac{61 \times 100\ (\text{Base})}{2} - 42$$

$$=\ 3050 - 42 = 3008$$

3.   46
        × 42

46	/	–	4
42	/	–	8
38	/	+	32

| Crosswise operation (46 – 8) or (42 – 4) gives us 38). |

$$\frac{38 \times 100 \text{ (Base)}}{2} + 32 = 1932$$

Problems:

(1)   63
        × 48
   _____

(2)   57
        × 52
   _____

(3)   58
        × 53
   _____

(4)   59
        × 47
   _____

(5)   58
        × 46
   _____

(6)   55
        × 63
   _____

(7)   46
        × 48
   _____

(8)   52
        × 47
   _____

(9)   68
        × 46
   _____

(10)   57
         × 46
   _____

Answers:

1. 3024   **2.** 2964   **3.** 3074   **4.** 2773

5. 2668   **6.** 3465   **7.** 2208   **8.** 2444

9. 3128   **10.** 2622

26

Multiplication of digits near 200

We have learned to multiply digits near 100 and 50 by using 'Quick Formula'. But does this formula hold good for digits near 200 also? Let us see.

Here:

1. The base is 100.
2. The difference of the digits is taken from 200.
3. $200 = 100 \times 2$
4. So we will multiply the digits obtained through crosswise operation by 2.

Example:

$$208$$
$$\times 211$$

208	/ +	8
211	/ +	11

Crosswise operation (208 + 11) gives us 219.

$$2 \times (219) \times (Base) / + 88 = 43888$$

You can verify this by other multiplication methods.
Let us take some more examples.

Example:

1.
$$212$$
$$\times 192$$

212	/ +	12
192	/ −	8

Crosswise operation (212−8) or (192+12) gives us 204.

$$2 \times 0 \ (204) \quad / - \quad 96$$

$$2 \times 204 \times (Base) / - 96$$
$$40800 - 96 = 40704$$

27

2.

$$
\begin{array}{r}
187 \\
\times\,184 \\
\end{array}
$$

187	/ –	13
184	/ –	16
171	/ +	208

Crosswise operation (187–16) or (184 – 13) gives us 171.

$2 \times (171) \times (Base) + 208$

$342 + 208 = 34408$

3.

$$
\begin{array}{r}
196 \\
\times\,182 \\
\end{array}
$$

196	/ –	4
182	/ –	18
178	/ +	72

Crosswise operation (196–18) or (182–4) gives us 178.

$2 \times (178) \times (Base) + / 72 = 35672$

Problems:

(1)
$$
\begin{array}{r}
206 \\
\times\,203 \\
\hline
\end{array}
$$

(2)
$$
\begin{array}{r}
212 \\
\times\,218 \\
\hline
\end{array}
$$

(3)
$$
\begin{array}{r}
197 \\
\times\,204 \\
\hline
\end{array}
$$

(4)
$$
\begin{array}{r}
186 \\
\times\,202 \\
\hline
\end{array}
$$

(5)
$$
\begin{array}{r}
197 \\
\times\,187 \\
\hline
\end{array}
$$

(6)
$$
\begin{array}{r}
184 \\
\times\,208 \\
\hline
\end{array}
$$

(7)
$$
\begin{array}{r}
216 \\
\times\,212 \\
\hline
\end{array}
$$

(8)
$$
\begin{array}{r}
209 \\
\times\,211 \\
\hline
\end{array}
$$

(9)
$$
\begin{array}{r}
202 \\
\times\,176 \\
\hline
\end{array}
$$

(10)
$$
\begin{array}{r}
182 \\
\times\,187 \\
\hline
\end{array}
$$

Answers:

1. 41818   2. 46216   3. 40188   4. 37572
5. 36839   6. 38272   7. 45792   8. 44099
9. 35552   10. 34034

Multiplication of digits near 150

You have learned Quick Formula for the multiplication of digits near 100, 50 and 200.

Now I will explain the formula for the multiplication of digits near 150.

Here:

1. The base is 100.

2. The difference of the digits is taken from 150.

3. $150 = 100 \times \frac{3}{2}$

4. So the multiplication factor will be $\frac{3}{2}$.

Let me explain this by an example:

$$\begin{array}{r} 162 \\ \times\, 148 \\ \hline \end{array}$$

162	/	+ 12
148	/	− 02
160	/	− 24

Crosswise operation
(162 − 2) or (148+12)
gives us 160.

The multiplication factor is $\frac{3}{2}$.

$160 \times \frac{3}{2} \times 100$ (Base) /- 24

$240 \times$ (Base) 100 /- 24

$24000 - 24 = 23976.$

Problems:

(1)   156
        × 158
_____

(2)   143
        × 152
_____

(3)   152
        × 144
_____

(4)   162
        × 156
_____

(5)   132
        × 152
_____

(6)   163
        × 161
_____

(7)   168
        × 143
_____

(8)   159
        × 144
_____

(9)   146
        × 148
_____

(10)   152
        × 161
_____

(11)   147
        × 146
_____

(12)   169
        × 142
_____

Answers:

1.	24648	**2.**	21736	**3.**	21888
4.	25272	**5.**	20064	**6.**	26243
7.	24024	**8.**	22896	**9.**	21608
10.	24472	**11.**	21462	**12.**	23998

The importance of bases in Quick Formula

How do we find the multiplication factor?
Simply, divide by the base = 100.

		Multiplication factor
Viz.	Digits near 100	1
	50	$\frac{1}{2}$
	200	2
	250	$\frac{5}{2}$
	300	3
	350	$\frac{7}{2}$
	400	4
	450	$\frac{9}{2}$
	500	5

Choice of bases

You can choose bases such as 10, 100 or 1000. The number of digits on the right-hand side of the slash will be equal to the number of zeros in the base.

Examples:

Base 10

1.
$$
\begin{array}{rr}
12 & \quad 12 \ / \ + \ 2 \\
\times 8 & \quad \underline{\ \ 8 \ / \ - \ 2} \\
& \quad 10 \ / \ - \ 4
\end{array}
$$

$$10 \times 10 \ (Base) - 4$$
$$100 - 4 = 96$$

2.
```
      9          9   /   − 1
    × 6          6   /   − 4
   ───        ─────────────
                5   /   + 4
```

or 5 × 10 (Base) + 4 = 54

Digits near multiples of 10 (i.e, 10, 20, 30, etc.)

Examples:

1.
```
     36        36   /   + 6
   × 32        32   /   + 2
   ────      ───────────────
               38   /      12
```

| Operating zone = 10 × 3 |
| Distance taken from 30 |

3 × 38 × 10 (Base) / + 12
1140 / + 12 = 1152

2.
```
     24        24   /   + 4
   × 16        16   /   − 4
   ────      ───────────────
               20   /   − 16
```

| Operating zone = 10 × 2 |
| Distance taken from 20 |

Multiplication factor = 2 × 20 × 10 (Base)/− 16
= 400 −16 = 384

Base 100   (We have seen a lot of examples in
Base 1000   the previous pages.)

Examples:

1.
```
     989       989   /   − 11
   × 1018      1018  /   + 18
   ─────     ─────────────────
               1007  /   −198
```

= 1007 × 1000 (Base) − 198
= 1007000 − 198 = 1006802

33

2.
$$
\begin{array}{ll}
982 & 982 \ / - \ 18 \\
\times\,987 & 987 \ / - \ 13 \\
\hline
& 969 \ / + \ 234 \\
& = 969234
\end{array}
$$

3.
$$
\begin{array}{ll}
1013 & 1013 \ / + \ 13 \\
\times\,1012 & 1012 \ / + \ 12 \\
\hline
& 1025 \ / \quad 156 \\
& = 1025156
\end{array}
$$

Digits near multiples of 1000

Near 500

Example – 1
$$
\begin{array}{r}
512 \\
\times\,498 \\
\hline
\end{array}
$$

In this case:

1. The base is 1000.

2. The difference of digits is taken from 500.

3. $500 = 1000 \times \dfrac{1}{2}$

4. So the multiplication factor becomes $\dfrac{1}{2}$.

5. The number of digits on the right hand side = the number of zeros in the base.

$$
\begin{array}{rr}
512 \ / + & 12 \\
\times\,498 \ / - & 2 \\
\hline
510 \ / - & 024
\end{array}
$$

$$
= \frac{1}{2} \times 510 \times 1000 \ (\text{base}) - 024
$$

$$
= 255000 - 024 = 254976
$$

34

Example - 2

$$\begin{array}{r} 1508 \\ \times\, 1512 \end{array}$$

$$\boxed{\begin{array}{l} \text{Operating zone} = \frac{3}{2} \times 1000 \\ \text{Distance taken from 1500} \end{array}}$$

Here the multiplication factor $= \frac{3}{2}$.

$$\begin{array}{rcr} 1508 & + & 8 \\ \times\, 1512 & - & 12 \\ \hline 1520 & / & 096^* \end{array}$$

$$= 3/2 \times 1520 \, / \, 096$$
$$= 2280 \, / \, 096$$
$$= 2280096$$

* The number of digits on the right-hand side of the slash is equal to the number of zeros in the base.

Problems:

(1)	36 × 28	**(2)**	44 × 36	**(3)**	25 × 32
(4)	15 × 24	**(5)**	516 × 508	**(6)**	498 × 516
(7)	487 × 512	**(8)**	512 × 508	**(9)**	1506 × 1514
(10)	2016 × 1982	**(11)**	2018 × 2012	**(12)**	1516 × 1486

Answers:

1. 1008	**2.** 1584	**3.** 800
4. 360	**5.** 262128	**6.** 256968
7. 249344	**8.** 260096	**9.** 2280084
10. 3995715	**11.** 4060216	**12.** 2252776

3. Criss-Cross Technique

You have learnt 'First Formula' and 'Quick Formula' before this. While learning the above you must have wondered what you would do when you are required to multiply dissimilar digits. When you have three, four or five digits multiplied by two or three digits. Do not worry. Learn the techniques provided under this heading which will surely help you solve any kind of multiplication you come across.

Multiplying two-digit numbers by two-digit numbers.

Let us start with an example, using the conventional approach:

$$
\begin{array}{r}
68 \\
\times\,48 \\
\hline
544 \\
272 \\
\hline
3264
\end{array}
$$

What are the steps we have taken?

- We multiplied 68 by 8 and wrote it in the first row (544).
- Then we multiplied 68 by 4 and wrote it below the first line, after leaving one space on the right.
- We added them, beginning with the rightmost digit.
- We got the answer = 3264.

How will you do it faster?

Let me provide you a formula:

$$
\begin{array}{r}
a \quad\ b \\
\times \quad x \quad\ y \\
\hline
ay \quad by \\
ax \quad bx \\
\hline
ax\ /\ (ay + bx)\ /\ by \\
Cross
\end{array}
$$

37

You are familiar with such kinds of multiplication. In algebra we do the multiplication as shown above. Let us take an example to show how we can incorporate the above formula in our multiplication exercises.

Example:

$$\begin{array}{r} 68 \\ \times\,48 \\ \hline \end{array}$$

Assuming numbers as letters we can write down the above example as shown below:

$$\begin{array}{cc} (a) & (b) \\ 6 & 8 \\ (x) & (y) \\ 4 & 8 \\ \hline \end{array}$$

ax / ay + bx / by

24 / 48 + 32 / 64

24 / 80 / 64

3264

How did we arrive at the figure 3264?

Steps:

- We started from the right, kept 4 as the digit on the extreme right and 6 as the remainder.
- The remainder 6 is added to the middle portion,

  80+6 = 86. We put 6 as the answer digit and 8 as the remainder.
- The remainder 8 is added to the digit on the extreme left, i.e 24 + 8 and we get 32 as the left part of the answer.
- Thus we get 3264 as the answer.

Let us take another example to check our understanding of the formula:

$$
\begin{array}{cc}
a & b \\
\times \quad x & y \\
\hline
ay & by \\
ax & bx \\
\hline
\end{array}
$$

ax / (ay + bx) /by
Cross

```
        76
      × 42
   ──────────
   28/14 + 24/12
   28/38/12 - Answer

   31  9  2
       3  1
```
–Remainder at each stage

Let us take another example to make our understanding crystal clear:

```
      87
   ×  68
   ─────────────
   48 / 64 + 42 / 56
       59   1   6    – Answer
           11   5    – Remainder at each stage
```

Have you understood the steps?

Can you do it now?

Try ……..

```
      76
   ×  52
   ─────────
   3952        – Answer
      4 1      – Remainder at each stage
```

Steps explained again:

- First multiply the digits on the right-6 and 2. It comes to 12. Put 2 as the answer digit and 1 as the remainder.
- Then multiply the numbers crosswise and add 14+30 = 44 (ay + bx); the remainder 1 is added to 44, and it becomes 45. Digit 5 is the answer and 4 is the remainder.
- Then multiply and add the remainder 4 to it —i.e. 7×5 (a x) = 35 + 4 = 39.
- The answer is 3952.

Steps explained again in short.
Right - Right, Cross, Left - Left.
Start from right

Some more examples:

(1)

$$67$$
$$\times 54$$
$$\overline{30 / 24+35 / 28}$$
$$3618$$

(2)

$$65$$
$$\times 77$$
$$\overline{42 / 42+35 / 35}$$
$$5005$$

(3)

$$24$$
$$\times 72$$
$$\overline{14 / 4 + 28/8}$$
$$1728$$

Problems:

(1) 76 × 19	**(2)** 77 × 24	**(3)** 67 × 23	**(4)** 64 × 29
(5) 83 × 28	**(6)** 86 × 27	**(7)** 73 × 77	**(8)** 79 × 37
(9) 94 × 24	**(10)** 34 × 62	**(11)** 44 × 64	**(12)** 83 × 23
(13) 78 × 76	**(14)** 75 × 74	**(15)** 77 × 79	**(16)** 80 × 87
(17) 66 × 68	**(18)** 71 × 93	**(19)** 19 × 72	**(20)** 74 × 64

Answers:

1. 1444	**2.** 1848	**3.** 1541	**4.** 1856
5. 2324	**6.** 2322	**7.** 5621	**8.** 2923
9. 2256	**10.** 2108	**11.** 2816	**12.** 1909
13. 5928	**14.** 5550	**15.** 6083	**16.** 6960
17. 4488	**18.** 6603	**19.** 1368	**20.** 4736

Multiplying three-digit numbers by two-digit numbers

You have learnt to multiply two-digit numbers by two-digit numbers. Did you notice the utility of the criss-cross technique?

Now, let us learn to multiply three-digit numbers by two-digit numbers.

I shall repeat the conventional method once again, just to make you aware of the difference.

```
        3  2  4
     ×  6  4
     ─────────
     1  2  9  6
  1  9  4  4
  ─────────────
  2  0  7  3  6
```

You are aware of the steps.

After seeing the conventional multiplication techniques, let us now turn towards the magical one.

I shall explain it to you using, a, b, c & x, y.

```
             a      b      c
          ×         x      y
          ───────────────────
             ay     by     cy
     ax      bx     cx
     ──────────────────────
     ax / ay + bx / by + cx / cy
         Cross    Cross
```

Let us compare this by the formula given for the multiplication of two-digit numbers by two digit numbers.

Do we notice some difference! Nothing much, only that one cross has increased.

In the two-digits by two-digits, there was only one cross—but here the number of crosses are two.

Now let us try to use the formula provided above, i.e.:

a	b	c
	x	y
ay	by	cy
ax	bx	cx

$$ax / ay + bx / by + cx / cy$$

a	b	c
3	2	7
	x	y
	4	2

12/ 6+8 / 4+28 / 14

= 13 7 3 4 - Answer

~~1 3 1~~ - Remainder at each stage

Let me explain the steps:

$$327$$
$$\times 42$$

Steps:

- We start from the right.
  $7 \times 2 = 14$, (cy). 4 is kept as the answer digit and 1 as the remainder.

- First cross (by + cx) = 4 + 28 = 32. When the remainder 1 is added to if, it becomes 33. Then 3 is kept as the answer and 3 as the remainder.

- Second cross (ay + bx) = 6 + 8 = 14. When the remainder 3 is added to it, it becomes 17. Then 7 is put as the answer digit and 1 is left as the remainder.

43

- Last operation (ax) gives us 12, remainder 1 is added to it (12 + 1 = 13), and 13 is put on the left of 7 as the answer digit.
- Thus we obtain the answer 13734.

Steps explained in short:

Right - Right, Cross - 1, Cross - 2, Left - Left.
Start from Right

Let us take some more examples to understand the formula more clearly:

$$3 \quad\quad 1 \quad\quad 7$$
$$\times \quad 7 \quad\quad 2$$
$$\overline{21 / 6 + 7 / 2 + 49 / 14}$$

or   22 8 2 4 - Answer
     ~~1 5 1~~ - Remainder at each stage.

The numbers shown below are the remainders left at each stage.

More examples:

1.   3 4 9
     × 6 4
$$\overline{18 / 12 + 24 / 16 + 54 / 36}$$

    22 3 3 6 - Answer
     ~~4 7 3~~ - Remainder at each stage

2.   6 9 3
     × 6 4
$$\overline{36 / 24 + 54 / 36 + 18 / 12}$$

    44 3 5 2 - Answer
     ~~8 5 1~~ - Remainder at each stage.

44

3.

$$
\begin{array}{r}
6\ 2\ 4 \\
\times\ 5\ 8 \\
\hline
30\ /\ 48 + 10\ /\ 16 + 20\ /\ 32
\end{array}
$$

36 1 9 2 - Answer
~~6 3 3~~ - Remainder at each stage.

Problems:

(1) 336 × 45	(2) 442 × 48	(3) 664 × 28	(4) 678 × 72
(5) 338 × 37	(6) 446 × 72	(7) 557 × 38	(8) 642 × 23
(9) 883 × 24	(10) 972 × 36	(11) 654 × 34	(12) 778 × 34
(13) 372 × 42	(14) 449 × 37	(15) 365 × 26	(16) 376 × 32
(17) 318 × 53	(18) 326 × 57	(19) 442 × 76	(20) 149 × 75

Answers:

1. 15120	2. 21216	3. 18592	4. 48816
5. 12506	6. 32112	7. 21166	8. 14766
9. 21192	10. 34992	11. 22236	12. 26452
13. 15624	14. 16613	15. 9490	16. 12032
17. 16854	18. 18582	19. 33592	20. 11175

Multiplying four-digit numbers by two-digit numbers

You have learnt to multiply two-digit numbers by other two-digit numbers and three-digit numbers by two-digit numbers.

Now we will learn to multiply four-digit numbers by two-digit numbers.

Let us do that:

Conventional method:

```
      4 2 7 3
     ×   2 4
   ───────────
    1 7 0 9 2
      8 5 4 6
   ───────────
  1 0 2 5 5 2
```

I am assuming that you are aware of the conventional approach and its complexity.

Let us do this by the criss-cross method. We will try it by using a, b, c, d and x, y.

```
       a    b    c    d
    ×            x    y
   ──────────────────────
      ay   by   cy   dy
   ax bx   cx   dx
  ────────────────────────
```
ax / ay + bx / by + cx / cy + dx / dy
    Cross   Cross   Cross

Let us solve a sum to understand the formula:

a b c d	4 3 7 6
× y	× 3 2

ax/ay+bx/by+cx/cy+dx/dy   12/8+9/6+21/14+18 12

Steps explained:

- Start from the right.
- $dy = 6 \times 2 = 12$, 2 is kept as the answer digit and the remainder is 1.
- $cy + dx = 14 + 18 = 32 + \text{remainder} = 32 + 1 = 33$, 3 is kept as the answer digit and the remainder is 3.
- $by + cx = 6 + 21 = 27 + \text{remainder} = 27 + 3 = 30$.

  0 is kept as the answer digit and the remainder is 3.
- $ay + bx = 8 + 9 = 17 + \text{remainder} = 17 + 3 = 20$,

  0 is kept as the answer digit and the remainder is 2.
- $ax = 12 + \text{remainder} = 12 + 2 = 14$.

  This completes the answer.
- The answer = 140032.

What is the difference between the four-digits × two-digits and the three-digits × two-digits. The difference is in the number of crosses. In the three-digits × two-digits the number of crosses were two, whereas here in this case it is three.

More examples:

1.

$$\begin{array}{r} 3\ 7\ 8\ 4 \\ \times\ 3\ 7 \\ \hline \end{array}$$

9/21+21/49+24/56+12/28

14 0 0 0 8 - Answer

~~5 8 7 2~~ - Remainder at each stage

2.

$$\begin{array}{r} 4\ 8\ 4\ 9 \\ \times\ 4\ 6 \\ \hline \end{array}$$

15/24+32/48+16/24+36/54

22 3 0 5 4 - Answer

~~6 7 6 5~~ - Remainder at each stage

47

Problems:

(1) 6336 × 42	**(2)** 6453 × 78	**(3)** 5742 × 64	**(4)** 4362 × 26
(5) 4564 × 66	**(6)** 6342 × 78	**(7)** 8236 × 32	**(8)** 9786 × 43
(9) 5347 × 37	**(10)** 6446 × 31	**(11)** 3236 × 54	**(12)** 2137 × 49

Answers:

1. 266112	**2.** 503334	**3.** 367488
4. 113412	**5.** 301224	**6.** 494676
7. 263552	**8.** 420798	**9.** 197839
10. 199826	**11.** 174744	**12.** 104713

48

Multiplying five-digit numbers by two-digit numbers.

You have learnt to multiply four-digit numbers by two-digit numbers

What have you understood? As you increase one-digit at the top, the number of crosses increases by one.

It means, here in this five-digits × two-digits the number of crosses will be one more than that in the four-digits × two-digits; Yes, you are right.

Let us write the formula:

$$
\begin{array}{ccccc}
a & b & c & d & e \\
  & \times & & x & y \\
\hline
ay & by & cy & dy & ey \\
ax & bx & cx & dx & ex \\
\hline
\end{array}
$$

ax / ay + bx / by + cx / cy + dx / dy + ex / ey
cross   cross   cross   cross

Let us solve a problem to have a clear understanding:

$$
\begin{array}{ccccc}
4 & 2 & 3 & 7 & 2 \\
 & & \times & 3 & 4 \\
\hline
\end{array}
$$

12 / 16 + 6 / 8 + 9 / 12 + 21 / 28 + 6 / 8

1 4 4 0 6 4 8 - Answer

~~2 2 3 3 0~~ - Remainder at each stage

Problems:

(1)	36742 × 36	**(2)**	27648 × 46	**(3)**	42373 × 63
(4)	37421 × 27	**(5)**	36842 × 42	**(6)**	87641 × 34

(7)	43458 × 34	**(8)**	34261 × 38	**(9)**	37649 × 23
(10)	21386 × 26	**(11)**	38312 × 36	**(12)**	87628 × 29
(13)	33429 × 54	**(14)**	45262 × 47		

Answers:

1. 1322712	**2.** 1271808	**3.** 2669499
4. 1010367	**5.** 1547364	**6.** 2979794
7. 1477572	**8.** 1301918	**9.** 865927
10. 556036	**11.** 1379232	**12.** 2541212
13. 1805166	**14.** 2427314	

Multiplying three-digit numbers by three-digit numbers.

You have learnt a lot of things in multiplication so far. Now you can create your own formulae for multiplication of any digit by two-digit numbers. Now we will try to learn to multiply three-digit numbers by three-digit numbers.

Let me start with the conventional approach just to show you the number of steps required to solve it:

```
          6 8 9
      ×   3 7 6
      _____
      4 1 3 4
    4 8 2 3
  2 0 6 7
  _____
  2 5 9 0 6 4
```

Steps explained:

1. First of all we multiplied 689 by 6 and wrote the answer in the first row (4134).

2. Then we multiplied 689 by 7 and wrote the answer in the second row, after leaving one space from the right (4823).

3. Then we multiplied 689 by 3 and wrote the digits below the second row, after leaving two spaces from the right (2067).

4. We then added them and got the answer as 259064.

Now let us try to see the faster method. We will again explain this method using a, b, c and x, y, z.

Let us start:

	a	b	c
×	x	y	z

		az	bz	cz
	ay	by	cy	
ax	bx	cx		

ax / ay + bx / az + by + cx / bz + cy / cz

2nd degree cross

If we compare this formula with the three-digit by two-digit formula, then we find that there is a change in the degree of crossing (third step from the right).

Let us solve one example using the above formula:

	6	3	4
×	7	4	6

42/24+21/36+28+12/18+16/24

= 47 2 9 6 4 - Answer
~~5 7 3 2~~ - Remainder

Let us try to solve some more sums keeping the formula in mind:

(1)

	8	7	9
×	3	4	2

24/32+21/16+27+28/14+36/18

30 0 6 1 8 - Answer
~~6 7 5 1~~ - Remainder

52

(2)
$$\begin{array}{r} 3\ \ 4\ \ 6 \\ \times\ 7\ \ 9\ \ 2 \\ \hline \end{array}$$

21/27+28/6+42+36/8+54/12

27 4 0 3 2   - Answer
~~6 9 6 1~~   - Remainder

(3)
$$\begin{array}{r} 5\ \ 7\ \ 8 \\ \times\ 6\ \ 4\ \ 3 \\ \hline \end{array}$$

30/20+42/15+48+28/21+32/24

37 1 6 5 4   - Answer
~~7 9 5 2~~   - Remainder

(4)
$$\begin{array}{r} 6\ \ 3\ \ 2 \\ \times\ 4\ \ 2\ \ 8 \\ \hline \end{array}$$

24/12+12/48+8+6/24+4/16

27 0 4 9 6   - Answer
~~3 6 2 1~~   - Remainder

Problems:

(1) 523 × 674	**(2)** 876 × 328	**(3)** 594 × 674	**(4)** 976 × 574
(5) 878 × 628	**(6)** 589 × 382	**(7)** 684 × 884	**(8)** 674 × 156

(9) 376 × 732	**(10)** 486 × 456	**(11)** 774 × 382	**(12)** 856 × 128

(13) 836 × 712	**(14)** 434 × 754	**(15)** 689 × 486	**(16)** 483 × 287

Answers:

1. 352502	**2.** 287328	**3.** 400356	**4.** 560224
5. 551384	**6.** 224998	**7.** 604656	**8.** 105144
9. 275232	**10.** 221616	**11.** 295668	**12.** 109568
13. 595232	**14.** 327236	**15.** 334854	**16.** 138621

Multiplying four-digit numbers by three-digit numbers.

Having learnt to multiply three-digit numbers by three-digit numbers, four-digit numbers by three-digit numbers is not difficult.

Everything remains the same, only a second degree cross increases by 1.

Let us solve:

$$
\begin{array}{cccc}
a & b & c & d \\
\times & x & y & z \\
\hline
az & bz & cz & dz \\
ay & by & cy & dy \\
ax & bx & cx & dx \\
\hline
\end{array}
$$

ax / ay + bx / az + by + cx / bz + cy + dx / cz + dy / dz
2nd degree cross   2nd degree cross

Let us solve an example, using this formula:

$$
\begin{array}{cccc}
4 & 3 & 7 & 2 \\
\times & 3 & 4 & 6 \\
\hline
\end{array}
$$

12/16+9/24+21+12/18+6+28/42+8/12

$= 15\ 1\ 2\ 7\ 1\ 2$ - Answer
$\ \ 3\ 6\ 5\ 5\ 1$ - Remainder at each stage

Let us solve some more examples keeping the formula in mind:

1.
$$
\begin{array}{cccc}
3 & 8 & 4 & 6 \\
\times & 2 & 1 & 6 \\
\hline
\end{array}
$$

6/3+16/18+8+8/48+12+4/24+6/36

$= 8\ 3\ 0\ 7\ 3\ 6$ - Answer
$\ 2\ 4\ 6\ 3\ 3$ - Remainder at each stage

55

2.

$$
\begin{array}{cccc}
5 & 2 & 6 & 4 \\
\times \quad 2 & 3 & 8 \\
\end{array}
$$

10/15+4/40+12+6/16+8+18/48+12/32

= 1 2 5 2 8 3 2 - Answer
~~2 6 4 6 3~~ - Remainder at each stage

Problems:

(1) 4632
$\times$ 347
_____

(2) 3647
$\times$ 573
_____

(3) 5321
$\times$ 132
_____

(4) 6821
$\times$ 418
_____

(5) 4513
$\times$ 476
_____

(6) 5732
$\times$ 563
_____

(7) 5744
$\times$ 347
_____

(8) 5857
$\times$ 637
_____

(9) 4843
$\times$ 743
_____

(10) 5844
$\times$ 634
_____

(11) 5896
$\times$ 347
_____

(12) 5949
$\times$ 743
_____

Answers:

1. 1607304 **2.** 2089731 **3.** 702372
4. 2851178 **5.** 2148188 **6.** 3227116
7. 1993168 **8.** 3730909 **9.** 3598349
10. 3705096 **11.** 2045912 **12.** 4420107

4. Mental Multiplication Techniques

Mental multiplication techniques will be helpful to you if you are planning to take competitive exams in the future. In competitive exams, problems are not difficult, say a lot of experts. It is the time constraint which makes all the difference. You are required to solve a lot of problems in a given time.

Now let me ask what you should you do to consume less time? Do the sums mentally.

Have you ever tried to take a print-out from a computer. If yes, then you must be knowing that print-processing takes seconds whereas printing on a paper takes a few minutes. Why so? Because processing by CPU is an electronic process whereas printing by a printer is a mechanical process. Much in the same manner, mental calculation is electronic and solving it on paper is mechanical. I hope you are able to understand this analogy.

Multiplying two-digit numbers by two-digit numbers

Let me explain the mental calculation technique:
The mental multiplication technique is based on the criss-cross technique. In the criss-cross technique, digits were written in an up and down order, whereas here, the digits are written in a row. You can use the same criss-cross formula to solve the example:

a b   x y   ax/ay+bx/by
3 6 × 2 4 = 6/12+12/24
    = 8 6 4 - Answer
      2 2 - Remainder at each stage

Steps explained:

- Assume 24 to be below 36 and multiply.
- Write the stagewise remainder at the bottom as shown.
- Work from right to left.

Let us do some more:

$$a\,b \times x\,y \qquad a\,x\,/\,a\,y + b\,x\,/\,b\,y$$

- $63 \times 74 = 46\ 6\ 2$ - Answer

  $4\ 1$ - Remainder at each stage

- $77 \times 23 = 17\ 7\ 1$ - Answer

  $3\ 2$ - Remainder at each stage

- $75 \times 64 = 48\ 0\ 0$ - Answer

  $6\ 2$ - Remainder at each stage

- $79 \times 83 = 65\ 5\ 7$ - Answer

  $9\ 2$ - Remainder at each stage

Problems:

(1) 78×64	**(2)** 67×56	**(3)** 35×47
(4) 46×73	**(5)** 47×52	**(6)** 33×39
(7) 77×34	**(8)** 63×28	**(9)** 71×26
(10) 68×54	**(11)** 98×23	**(12)** 74×29

Answers:

1. 4992	**2.** 3752	**3.** 1645
4. 3358	**5.** 2444	**6.** 1287
7. 2618	**8.** 1764	**9.** 1846
10. 3672	**11.** 2254	**12.** 2146

Multiplying three-digit numbers by two-digit numbers

After learning mental multiplication of two-digit numbers by two-digit numbers, let us proceed to three-digit numbers by two-digit numbers.

Let us start with examples:

$$abc \qquad xy \qquad ax/ay+bx/by+cx/cy$$

- $336 \times 62 = 20 \ 8 \ 3 \ 2$ - Answer

  $2 \ 4 \ 1$ - Remainder at each stage

- $472 \times 24 = 11 \ 3 \ 2 \ 8$ - Answer

  $3 \ 3 \ 0$ - Remainder at each stage

- $638 \times 32 = 20 \ 4 \ 1 \ 6$ - Answer

  $2 \ 3 \ 1$ - Remainder at each stage

- $436 \times 56 = 24 \ 4 \ 1 \ 6$ - Answer

  $4 \ 5 \ 3$ - Remainder at each stage

- $538 \times 64 = 34 \ 4 \ 3 \ 2$ - Answer

  $4 \ 6 \ 3$ - Remainder at each stage

- $654 \times 54 = 35 \ 3 \ 1 \ 6$ - Answer

  $5 \ 4 \ 1$ - Remainder at each stage

Problems:

(1) 678×52	**(2)** 272×36	**(3)** 853×44
(4) 422×73	**(5)** 584×46	**(6)** 346×28
(7) 921×28	**(8)** 841×83	**(9)** 673×49
(10) 674×59	**(11)** 371×31	**(12)** 849×47

Answers:

1. 35256	**2.** 9792	**3.** 37532
4. 30806	**5.** 26864	**6.** 9688
7. 25788	**8.** 69803	**9.** 32977
10. 39766	**11.** 11501	**12.** 39903

Multiplying four-digit numbers by two-digit numbers

Just now you have learnt to multiply three-digit numbers by two-digit numbers mentally. Now let me explain mental multiplication of four-digits by two digits.

Let us start with examples:

a b c d xy   ax/ay+bx/by+cx/cy+dx/dy

- $4235 \times 24 = 10\,1640$ - Answer
  - ~~2122~~   - Remainder at each stage

- $6742 \times 64 = 43\,1488$ - Answer
  - ~~7520~~   - Remainder at each stage

- $8742 \times 76 = 66\,4392$ - Answer
  - ~~10731~~   - Remainder at each stage

- $6453 \times 82 = 52\,9146$ - Answer
  - ~~4530~~   - Remainder at each stage

Problems:

(1) 6337×53	**(2)** 5757×43	**(3)** 6742×34
(4) 4321×27	**(5)** 4476×29	**(6)** 3842×37
(7) 4874×72	**(8)** 5833×82	**(9)** 9647×83
(10) 9949×29	**(11)** 8764×53	**(12)** 7323×82

Answers:

1. 335861	**2.** 247551	**3.** 229228
4. 116667	**5.** 129804	**6.** 142154
7. 350928	**8.** 478306	**9.** 800701
10. 288521	**11.** 464492	**12.** 600486

Multiplying five-digit numbers by two-digit numbers

Hopefully you have understood by now, how to mentally multiply four-digits by two-digits. Let us now learn to mentally multiply five-digits by two-digits.

Let us start with examples:

abcde × xy   ax/ay+bx/by + cx/cy+dx/dy+ex/ey

• 64327 × 74 = 47 6 0 1 9 8 - Answer
                 5 4 3 5 2 - Remainder at each stage

• 38743 × 27 =10 4 6 0 6 1 - Answer
                4 7 6 3 2 - Remainder at each stage

Problems:

(1) 64389×47	**(2)** 34673×28	**(3)** 32576 × 34
(4) 37426×31	**(5)** 52764×41	**(6)** 87621 × 35·
(7) 41312×31	**(8)** 31761× 36	**(9)** 52173 × 39
(10) 51342×51	**(11)** 21224×53	**(12)** 62173 × 82

Answers:

1. 3026283	**2.** 970844	**3.** 1107584
4. 1160206	**5.** 2163324	**6.** 3066735
7. 1280672	**8.** 1143396	**9.** 2034747
10. 2618442	**11.** 1124872	**12.** 5098186

If you have really understood the fundamentals so far, then you can multiply and create your own formulae for the following:

six-digits $\times$ two-digits

seven-digits $\times$ two-digits

eight-digits $\times$ two-digits

nine-digits $\times$ two-digits

Multiplying three-digit numbers by three-digit numbers

You have learned to mentally multiply upto five-digit numbers by two-digit numbers. Mental multiplication of three-digit numbers by three-digit numbers should not be difficult for you any more.

Let us start with an example:

$$a\,b\,c \quad x\,y\,z \quad ax/ay+bx/az+by+cx/bz+cy/cz$$

- $542 \times 236 = 12\,7\,9\,1\,2$ - Answer

  $2\,4\,3\,1$ - Remainder at each stage

- $473 \times 324 = 15\,3\,2\,5\,2$ - Answer

  $3\,4\,3\,1$ - Remainder at each stage

Problems:

(1) 573×284	**(2)** 642×473	**(3)** 852×341
(4) 971×488	**(5)** 952×217	**(6)** 672×499
(7) 871×273	**(8)** 856×262	**(9)** 947×376
(10) 948×487	**(11)** 864×623	**(12)** 761×671

Answers:

1.	162732	**2.**	303666	**3.**	290532
4.	473848	**5.**	206584	**6.**	335328
7.	237783	**8.**	224272	**9.**	356072
10.	461676	**11.**	538272	**12.**	510631

Division

1. Real Magic

I am certain that you will be thrilled after learning and understanding these methods. You will find this magical. Also you will find this very easy to work with. Try to teach these methods to as many people as you can.

Denominator ending with 9

Find $\frac{73}{139}$ up to 5 places of decimal. Let us try to solve it first by the conventional method:

```
139 )  730  ( 0.5 2 5 1 7
       695
       ────
       350
       278
       ────
       720
       695
       ────
       250
       139
       ────
      1110
       973
       ────
       137
```

Now, let us see the magical method:

$$\frac{73}{139} = \frac{7.3}{13.9} = \frac{7.3}{14} = 0 \,.\, 5 \quad 2 \quad 5 \quad 1 \quad 7 \quad \text{- Answer}$$

$$\phantom{\frac{73}{139} = 0 \,.\,} \cancel{3 \quad 7 \quad 2 \quad 11} \quad \text{- Remainder}$$

Check, whether both the answers are the same (?)

By the conventional method our answer to 5 places of decimal is 0.52517.

By the magical method too, our answer is 0.52517.

There is no difference in the answers. However, the procedure adopted in both the methods is different. One is more cumbersome than the other. Let me explain the steps.

Steps:

- 73 is divided by 139 (a digit ending with 9).

- $\frac{73}{139}$ is reduced to $\frac{7.3}{13.9}$ or $\frac{7.3}{14}$

- Start dividing 73 by 14.

- Put the decimal point first; divide 73 by 14. 5 is the quotient and 3 is the remainder. 5 is written after the decimal and 3 is written in front of 5 as shown below.

- Our next gross number is 35; divide 35 by 14. Quotient = 2 and remainder = 7. Q = 2 is written after 5 and R = 7 before 2 (below it).

- Our next gross number is 72; divide 72 by 14. Q = 5 and R = 2, Q = 5 is written after 2 and R = 2 before 5 (below it).

- Our next gross number is 25; divide 25 by 14. Quotient = 1 and remainder = 11. Q = 1 is written after 5 and R = 11 before 1 (below it).

- We have already found the answer up to four decimal places; our next dividend is 111 which is to be divided by 14. Quotient = 7, and thereby we have found the answer up to five places of decimal.

- Repeat the above steps if you want to find the values further.

You have learned the steps required to solve such kind of problems where the denominator ends with 9. Let us look at some more examples.

Examples:

- $\frac{75}{139} = \frac{7.5}{13.9} = \frac{75}{14} =$ 0. 5 3 9 5 6 8 - Answer

                    5 13 7 9 11 - Remainder

- $\frac{63}{149} = \frac{6.3}{14.9} = \frac{6.3}{15} = 0.4$ 2 2 8 1 8 7 - Answer

               3 4 12 2 13 11 - Remainder

- $\frac{83}{189} = \frac{8.3}{19} =$ = 0. 4 3 9 1 5 3 - Answer

             7 17 2 10 6 8 - Remainder

Problems:

(1) $\frac{76}{139}$		**(2)** $\frac{64}{129}$		**(3)** $\frac{1}{19}$	
(4) $\frac{1}{29}$		**(5)** $\frac{3}{39}$		**(6)** $\frac{5}{49}$	
(7) $\frac{63}{129}$		**(8)** $\frac{43}{179}$		**(9)** $\frac{83}{119}$	
(10) $\frac{76}{189}$		**(11)** $\frac{53}{149}$		**(12)** $\frac{57}{159}$	

Answers:

1.	0.54676	**2.**	0.49612	**3.**	0.052631
4.	0.034482	**5.**	0.076923	**6.**	0.1020408
7.	0.48837	**8.**	0.24022	**9.**	0.697478
10.	0.4021164	**11.**	0.3557046	**12.**	0.358490

Denominator ending with 8

You must be wondering whether the process explained is applicable only if a denominator ends with 9. The answer is no. We can apply this technique to digits that end with 8, 7, 6, etc., but with a slight change.

Let us see it applied to denominators ending with 8:

$$\frac{73}{138} = \frac{7.3}{13.8} = \frac{7.3}{14} = \overset{+5+2\ +8+9}{0.5\ 2\ 8\ 9\ 8} \text{ - Answer}$$

$$3\ \ 12\ 12\ 10 \text{ - Remainder}$$

In case of denominator digits ending with 8 (one less than 9), the steps are as follows:

1. Placing of the remainder in front of the quotient remains the same as explained in the case $\frac{73}{138}$ or where the denominator digit ends with 9.

2. In the quotient digit, 1 time $(9 - 8 = 1)$ of the quotient digit is added at every step and divided by the divisor for finding out the answer.

As in this case, we found our first Q1 = 5 and R1 = 3. Our gross dividend comes out to be 35 in which we added 5 to make it 40, then divided it by 14. In the next step Q2 = 2 and R2 = 12. Our gross dividend at step 2 becomes 122 + Q2 = 124. Divide this by 14.

68

The procedure is repeated to find the solution to the required number of decimal places.

Let us take some more examples so that we can understand it better:

1. $\dfrac{75}{168} = \dfrac{7.5}{16.8} = \dfrac{7.5}{17} = 0.\overset{+4+4+6+4+2}{4\ 4\ 6\ 4\ 2\ 8}$
   $\underset{7\ 10\ 6\ 4\ 14}{\ }$

2. $\dfrac{83}{178} = \dfrac{8.3}{17.8} = \dfrac{8.3}{18} = 0.\overset{+4+6+6+2}{4\ \ 6\ \ 6\ 2\ 9}$
   $\underset{11\ 10\ \ 4\ \ 16}{\ }$

3. $\dfrac{31}{188} = \dfrac{3.1}{18.8} = \dfrac{3.1}{19} = 0.\overset{+1+6+4+8}{1\ 6\ 4\ 8\ 9}$
   $\underset{12\ 8\ 16\ 16}{\ }$

Problems:

(1) $\dfrac{78}{138}$ (2) $\dfrac{74}{148}$ (3) $\dfrac{63}{128}$ (4) $\dfrac{51}{118}$

(5) $\dfrac{56}{118}$ (6) $\dfrac{49}{128}$ (7) $\dfrac{83}{178}$ (8) $\dfrac{89}{148}$

(9) $\dfrac{32}{148}$ (10) $\dfrac{37}{168}$

Answers:

1. 0.565217	2. 0.5	3. 0.492187
4. 0.43220	5. 0.474576	6. 0.38281
7. 0.466292	8. 0.601351	9. 0.216216
10. 0.22023		

Denominator ending with other digits:

After learning this magical method for denominator digits ending with 8, you would like to learn the same for denominator digits ending with 7.

Let me take one example:

$$\frac{73}{137} = \frac{7.3}{13.7} = \frac{7.3}{14} = 0. \underset{\underline{3\ \ \ 3\ \ 11\ \ 4\ \ \ 6}}{\overset{+\ 10 + 6 + 4 + 16 + 8}{5\ \ \ 3\ \ \ 2\ \ \ 8\ \ \ 4}}$$

Once you see the operation you know instantaneously that in this case the quotient digit is multiplied by 2 $(9 - 2 = 2)$ and added to the quotient. All other operations remains the same as before.

Can you guess what happens in case the denominator digit ends in 6?

$$\text{Say,}\ \frac{73}{136} = \frac{7.3}{14} = 0. \underset{\underline{3\ \ 8\ \ 8\ \ 6}}{\overset{+15+9+18+21}{5\ \ \ 3\ \ 6\ \ 7\ \ 6}}$$

In this case, three times the of Q digit has been added $(9-6=3)$.

Till now you have seen explanations of the following:

$$\frac{73}{139},\quad \frac{73}{138},\quad \frac{73}{137},\quad \frac{73}{136}$$

What will you do in the case of:

$$\frac{73}{135}\quad \frac{73}{134}\quad \frac{73}{133}\quad \frac{73}{132}\quad \text{and}\quad \frac{73}{131}?$$

Let us take the above mentioned cases one by one:

$\frac{73}{135}$ Multiply the numerator and the denominator by 2 to get the answer:

$$\frac{73}{135} \times \frac{2}{2} = \frac{146}{270} = \frac{146}{270} = \frac{1}{10} \times \frac{146}{27}$$

$\frac{73}{134}$ Multiply the numerator and the denominator by 5 to reduce the divisor:

$$\frac{73}{134} \times \frac{5}{5} = \frac{365}{670} = \frac{1}{10} \times \frac{365}{67}$$

$\frac{73}{133}$ Multiply the numerator and the denominator by 3. Apply the principle explained for the denominator ending with 9:

$$\frac{73}{133} \times \frac{3}{3} = \frac{219}{399} = \frac{21.9}{39.9} = \frac{21.9}{40} = 0.\,5\ 4\ 8\ 8\ 7$$
$$ \cancel{19\ 35\ 34\ 28\ 8}$$

$\frac{73}{132}$ Multiply the numerator and the denominator by 5 to reduce the divisor:

$$\frac{73}{132} \times \frac{5}{5} = \frac{365}{660} = \frac{1}{1} \times \frac{365}{66}$$

$\frac{73}{131}$ This case is slightly different here. We reduce 1 from both numerator and denominator.

$$\frac{73-1}{131-1} = \frac{72}{130} = \frac{7.2}{13} = \frac{7.2}{13} = 0.\,5\ 5\ 7\ 2$$
$$ 4\ 4\ 2\ 7$$
$$ \cancel{7\ 9\ 3\ 6}$$

In this case we proceed as explained before, but our gross dividend changes.

71

Earlier our gross dividend used to be the *remainder quotient*. Here in this case our gross dividend is the *remainder* (9 − quotient).

As shown in the example, our first gross number should have been 75, but it is 7 (9 − 5) = 74.

Let me take a few examples:

$$\frac{63}{121} = \frac{63-1}{121-1} = \frac{62}{120} = \frac{6.2}{12} = 0.\underset{2\ 0\ 7\ 7\ 1}{\overset{4\ 7\ 9\ 3}{5\ 2\ 0\ 6\ 6}}$$

$$\frac{59}{171} = \frac{5.8}{17} = 0.\underset{7\ 8\ 0\ 4\ 15}{\overset{6\ 5\ 4\ 9\ 7}{3\ 4\ 5\ 0\ 2\ 9}}$$

Numerator having more than one digit after the decimal

Will we be able to apply the same technique when digits after the decimal is more than 1 ?

Say, $\frac{738}{1399} = \frac{7.38}{13.99} = \frac{7.38}{14} = 0.\,52\,/\,75\,/$
$$10\ /\ 2$$

In the case explained above, we bring the remainder forward, after completion of two operations.

Now you will ask me what shall we do when the number of digits after the decimal places are three. We should bring the remainder forward after the completion of three operations.

Everything remains the same as explained earlier, only the operation related to the remainder changes.

Problems:

(1) $\frac{73}{131}$ (2) $\frac{84}{151}$ (3) $\frac{87}{171}$ (4) $\frac{89}{181}$ (5) $\frac{683}{1499}$

(6) $\frac{498}{1299}$ (7) $\frac{85}{176}$ (8) $\frac{45}{127}$ (9) $\frac{63}{137}$ (10) $\frac{54}{136}$

Answers:

1. 0.557251	**2.** 0.55629	**3.** 0.50877
4. 0.491712	**5.** 0.425617	**6.** 0.383371
7. 0.482954	**8.** 0.35433	**9.** 0.459854
10. 0.397058		

2. Criss-Cross Technique

Division format

The conventional format for division:

Divisor) Dividend (Quotient
$\underline{\qquad}$
Remainder

The magical format for division:

Flag | Dividend

Divisor $\underline{\qquad}$

Quotient : Remainder

Let us take an example to clarify:

178) 3246738 (

Quotient side
↓

Flag → 8 | 324673 : 8 ← Remainder side
Divisor → 17

Quotient : Remainder

Some finer points that need to be taken care of:

- Number of digits on the remainder side is always equal to the number of digits in the flag.
- The digits on the extreme right of the divisor is taken as the flag digit.

In the example shown above we have kept 8 as the flag digit. We will be dividing the dividend by the divisor 17.

You will ask me why I should adopt this format when I have a well tested conventional format. Here, I have to say that by the conventional format, division by small two-digit numbers is easy but when it comes to larger divisors it becomes inefficient. In this format we reduce large divisors to smaller ones. A four-digit divisor can be reduced to a two-digit or a one-digit divisor, thereby reducing the complicated process of multiplication involving large divisors.

Division of a number by a smaller three-digit number (Flag digit = 1)

One complete cycle of division is given by "Division + Direction", i.e. division by the divisor and direction from the flag.

Let us see how:

8	32	4	6 7 3 : 8
17		15	10
		18	

Steps:
Division by Divisor '17' + Direction from flag '8'.

- *Division*
  Our first digit for division is 32. 17 will go once in 32. The remainder is 15. 1 is written in the space reserved for the answer and 15 is written before 4, as shown. We will now seek directions from the flag digit, as our division by divisor step is over.

75

- *Direction*

  Our next gross dividend is 154. As part of the direction, multiply the first answer digit with the flag digit and then subtract from the gross dividend.

  $(154 - 8 \times 1 = 146)$. Our next dividend which will be divided by 17 is 146.

- *Division*

  Divide 146 by 17; it goes 8 times. Put 8 in the answer space after 1 and the remainder 10 before 6 as shown:

	8		32	4		6 7 3 : 8
	17			15	10	
				18		

- *Direction*

  Our gross dividend is 106. After taking direction $(106 - 8 \times 8 = 106 - 64 = 42)$, we are left with 42, which will be divided by 17.

- *Division*

  Divide 42 by 17; it goes 2 times. Put 2 in the answer space after 8 and the remainder 8 before 7 as shown:

	8	32	4	6	73 : 8
	17		15	10	8	
			182		

- *Direction*

  Our gross dividend is 87. Seek direction $[87 - (8 \times 2) = 71]$, the digit which will be further divided by 17.

76

- *Division*

  Divide 71 by 17. It can go 4 times. Put 4 in the answer place after 2, and the remainder 3 before 3 as shown:

8	32	4	6	7	3	:	8
17		15	10	8	3		
		1824					

- *Direction*

  Our gross dividend is 33. After seeking direction [(33-32) = 1], we are left with 1.

- *Division*

  Divide 1 by 17; 17 will go 0 times. Put 0 in the answer place and the remainder 1 before 8 in the remainder column as shown:

8	32	4	6	7	3	:	8
17		15	10	8	3	1	
		18240					

- *Direction*

  $18 - 0 \times 8 = 18$, remainder = 18.

  Our answer is 18240 and the remainder is 18.

Salient points revised:

- One complete operation involves division + direction.
- If after taking direction, you obtain a negative number, then reduce 1 from the previous quotient digit and work again.

Let me illustrate it by an example:

8	32	4	6	6	7	3	:	8
17		15	10	8	2			
	1824							

Steps:

- $32 \div 17 = Q = 1, R = 15$
- Gross dividend 154, take direction $15 - 8 \times 1 = 146$.
- $146 \div 17 = Q = 8, R = 10$.
- Gross dividend 106, take direction $106 - 64 = 42$.
- $42 \div 17 = Q = 2, R = 8$.
- Gross dividend 86, take direction $86 - 16 = 70$
- *Division*
  $70 \div 17 = Q = 4, R = 2$.
- *Direction*
  Gross dividend 27, after direction
  $27 - 8 \times 4 = [-5]$

Here we see that the answer is–5 after seeking direction. As this is a negative number, we cannot proceed further.

As explained earlier, we will go back and reduce the Q digit by 1, i.e.:

$70 \div 17 = Q = 3, R = 19$.

8	32	4	6	6	7	3	:	8
17		15	10	8	19	20		12
	182397	:	72					

- Gross digit 197, take direction 197 − 24 = 173.
- 173 ÷ 17 = Q = 9, R = 20. Here we are keeping Q=9 for the reason explained in the previous step.
- Gross digit 203, take direction 203 − 72 = 131.
- 131 ÷ 17 = Q = 7, R = 12.
- Gross digit on remainder side is 128, take direction 128 − 56 = 72. Our answer is 182397 and the remainder is 72.

After this long explanation, I can now hope that the division steps, will be clear to you. I had taken an extra long example only to drive the point home. Now, we will work with smaller examples.

1.

    156) 48764 (

Let us make our format.

6	48	7	6	:	4
15		3	4	10	
	312 : 92				

Q = 312
R = 92

1.
    37
− 18
―――
    19

2.
    46
− 6
―――
    40

3.
  104
− 12
―――
   92

2.

$73284 \div 187$

7	73	2	8	:	4
18		19	9		17

391 : 167

$Q = 391,$

$R = 167$

1.

$$\begin{array}{r} 192 \\ -\ 21 \\ \hline 171 \\ -\ 162 \\ \hline 9 \end{array}$$

Note:

If you have to divide by a large two-digit number say $6898 \div 89$, then you can make use of the format given below:

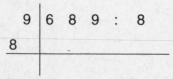

9 | 6 8 9 : 8

8

One digit as the flag digit (right one). One digit as the divisor (left one).

Problems:

(1)	$40897 \div 167$	**(2)**	$50326 \div 132$
(3)	$326312 \div 157$	**(4)**	$46896 \div 217$
(5)	$58919 \div 159$	**(6)**	$61312 \div 138$
(7)	$32163 \div 126$	**(8)**	$12462 \div 138$
(9)	$13662 \div 116$	**(10)**	$86962 \div 184$
(11)	$62123 \div 154$	**(12)**	$12633 \div 173$
(13)	$83448 \div 137$	**(14)**	$47132 \div 113$

(15)	87634÷198	(16)	48321÷164
(17)	58621÷189	(18)	32362÷98
(19)	58632÷89	(20)	62361÷167
(21)	13623÷158	(22)	12238÷78
(23)	21234÷97	(24)	63212÷169

Answers:

(1)	Q=244,	R=149	(2)	Q=381,	R=34
(3)	Q=2078,	R=66	(4)	Q=216,	R=24
(5)	Q=370,	R=89	(6)	Q=444,	R=40
(7)	Q=255,	R=33	(8)	Q=90,	R=42
(9)	Q=117,	R-90	(10)	Q=472,	R=114
(11)	Q=403,	R=61	(12)	Q=73,	R=4
(13)	Q=609,	R=15	(14)	Q=417,	R=11
(15)	Q=442,	R=118	(16)	Q=294,	R=105
(17)	Q=310,	R=31	(18)	Q=330,	R=22
(19)	Q=658,	R=70	(20)	Q=373,	R=70
(21)	Q=86,	R=35	(22)	Q=156,	R=70
(23)	Q=218,	R=88	(24)	Q=374,	R=6

Division of a number by a larger three-digit number (Flag digit = 2)

Now I will explain what happens when the divisor number is extra large. Say,

$$884) \; 3 \; 7 \; 4 \; 2 \; 6 \; 8 \; ($$

In such cases we put two digits in the flag and one digit as divisor as shown below:

```
84 | 3  7  4  2  :  6  8
 8 |       5  6
   |————————————————————
   |    4  2
```

I will explain the working procedure step by step:

- *Division*
  After making the format, divide the first gross digit 37 by 8. It goes 4 times and leaves a remainder= 5.

- *Direction*
  Next gross dividend is 54, take direction . Subtract "Left digit of the flag × First digit of quotient digit i.e. 54–(8 × 4) = 54 – 32 = 22.

- *Division*
  Next dividend for division is 22, which when divided by 8, goes 2 times , R = 6.

- *Direction*
  The gross dividend is 62. For direction, subtract cross of the flag digit with quotient digit.

i.e.　　$62 - [(8×2) + (4×4)]$

　　$= 62 - [16+16]$

　　$= 62 - [32]$

　　$= 30$

- *Division*

  Now the dividend is 30, which when divided by 8 goes 3 times, R = 6.

```
84 | 3 7 4 2 : 6 8
 8 |     5 6     6
   |_____
   |   4 2 3 :
```

- *Direction*

  Remainder 6 has been placed towards the remainder side.

Here the direction steps will be:

- Gross dividend is 66; we will subtract the cross of the flag digit and quotient:

i.e.　　　　66
　　　　　$- 32$
　　　　　$\overline{34}$

This comes to 34.

- The last dividend digit 8 will be placed on 34 and it becomes 348 from which we will subtract "Last flag digit × Last quotient digit",

  i.e. $348 - (4 \times 3) = 348 - 12 = 336$.

  Remainder = 336.

  Answer = 423 and remainder = 336.

Problems:

(1) $80649 \div 984$	**(2)** $60312 \div 762$	**(3)** $51336 \div 862$
(4) $4312 \div 978$	**(5)** $61231 \div 869$	**(6)** $78632 \div 789$
(7) $13263 \div 876$	**(8)** $76321 \div 594$	**(9)** $68323 \div 964$
(10) $89033 \div 879$	**(11)** $50321 \div 972$	**(12)** $99631 \div 997$

Answers:

(1) Q=81, R=945	**(2)** Q=79, R=114
(3) Q=59, R=478	**(4)** Q=44, R=180
(5) Q=70, R=401	**(6)** Q=99, R=521
(7) Q=15, R=123	**(8)** Q=128, R=289
(9) Q=70, R=843	**(10)** Q=101, R=254
(11) Q=51, R=749	**(12)** Q=99, R=928

Division of a number by a four-digit number.

By using two digits in the flag we can divide any number by four digits.

Let us see how;

Example:

827476 ÷ 1568

Let us make our format:

68	82 7 4 : 7 6	
15	7 17 17	
	527 : 1140	

(Step-1)   77
        − 30
        _____
           47

Steps:

- Division 82÷ 15; Q=5, R=7
- Direction 77 − (6 × 5) = 47
- Division 47÷15; Q = 2, R = 17
- Direction 174 − [(6×2)+(8×5)]=122

(Step-2)   174
        −   52
        _____
           122

(Step-3)   177
        −   58
        _____
          1196
        −   56
        _____
          1140

- Division 122÷15; Q=7, R=17
- Direction 177−cross = 119. Last dividend digit 6 will be placed on this.

1196 − [Last flag digit × last quotient digit]

1196 − [8 × 7] = 1140 (remainder)

Quotient = 627

Remainder = 1140

85

Problems:

(1)	106356 ÷ 1274		**(2)**	987634 ÷ 1156
(3)	382123 ÷ 1584		**(4)**	63426 ÷ 1376
(5)	87342 ÷ 1897		**(6)**	87643 ÷ 1654
(7)	38321 ÷ 1997		**(8)**	16841 ÷ 1764
(9)	18432 ÷ 1964		**(10)**	68432 ÷ 1843
(11)	81762 ÷ 1643		**(12)**	46421 ÷ 1732
(13)	38347 ÷ 1549		**(14)**	28614 ÷ 1963
(15)	56498 ÷ 1859		**(16)**	56432 ÷ 2136
(17)	38413 ÷ 1269		**(18)**	338624 ÷ 1781
(19)	64321 ÷ 1843		**(20)**	20016 ÷ 1836

Answers:

(1)	Q=83, R=614		**(2)**	Q=854, R=410
(3)	Q=241, R=379		**(4)**	Q=46, R=130
(5)	Q=46, R=80		**(6)**	Q=52, R=1635
(7)	Q=19, R=378		**(8)**	Q=9, R=965
(9)	Q=9, R=756		**(10)**	Q=37, R=241
(11)	Q=49, R=1255		**(12)**	Q=26, R=1389
(13)	Q=24, R=1171		**(14)**	Q=14, R=1132
(15)	Q=30, R=728		**(16)**	Q=26, R=896
(17)	Q=30, R=343		**(18)**	Q=190, R=234
(19)	Q=34, R=1659		**(20)**	Q=10, R=1656

Decimal division

Having discussed so much on division, let us now work to find the result up to a few places of decimals instead of remainders. Say we want to find 3246738 ÷ 178 up to 3 places of decimal.

Let us make our division format:

```
 8 | 3 2 4 6 7 3 : 8 : : 0 0 0
17 |
   |
```

Everything remains the same as explained earlier. Here, we have only added three extra zeros to solve it up to three places of decimals. We will have to solve this also as we did earlier.

(1)

```
 8 | 3 2  4  6  7 3 : 8 : :  0 0 0
17 |    15 10  8  3   1      1 2 3
   | 18240 . 101
```

```
 154
 - 8
 ───
 146
```

Steps explained:

- Division $32 \div 17$; $Q = 1$, $R = 15$
- Direction   gross dividend = 154,
  take direction $154 - 8 \times 1 = 146$
  $146 \div 17 = Q = 8$, $R = 10$
- Gross dividend 106,
  Direction, $106 - 64 = 42$
- $42 \div 17 = Q = 2$, $R = 8$
- Gross dividend 87,
  Direction $87 - 16 = 71$
- $71 \div 17 = Q = 4$, $R = 3$
- Gross dividend 33,
  Direction $33 - 32 = 1$
- $1 \div 17 = Q = 0$, $R = 1$

$$
\begin{array}{r}
\textbf{(2)} \quad 106 \\
- 64 \\
\hline
42 \\
\textbf{(3)} \quad 87 \\
- 16 \\
\hline
71 \\
\textbf{(4)} \quad 33 \\
- 32 \\
\hline
1 \\
\textbf{(5)} \quad 18 \\
- 0 \\
\hline
18 \\
\textbf{(6)} \quad 10 \\
- 8 \\
\hline
2
\end{array}
$$

We have entered into the remainder zone now, so we will put a decimal after the digits found so far as part of the answer.

- Gross dividend 18, direction $18 - 0 \times 8 = 18$
- $18 \div 17$, $Q = 1$, $R = 1$
- Gross dividend 10, direction $10 - (1 \times 8) = 2$
- $2 \div 17$, $Q = 0$, $R = 2$
- Gross dividend 20, direction $20 - 0 \times 8 = 20$
- $20 \div 17 = Q = 1$, $R = 3$.
- Gross dividend 30, direction $30 - 1 \times 8 = 22$. The answer is 18240.101

We can use the same technique for finding answers in decimals, for divisions involving three or four-digit numbers.

How to make the format for decimal division?

- If you are required to divide up to one decimal place, then the following format is applicable.
  86432 ÷ 197

7	8 6 4 3 : 2 : 0 ←	One zero is added here as we have to find the answer to one decimal place.
19		

- Suppose the answer required is up to two places of decimal, then our format will look like the following:

7	8 6 4 3 : 2 :0 0 ←	Two zeros have been added here to find the answer to two decimal places
19		

- Now, suppose you have to find the answer up to five decimal places, what will you do? You will add five zeros to the right of the dividend and divide the whole operation following the division procedure explained earlier. You will put the decimal sign as soon as you enter the remainder zone.

Problems:

Find the answer upto four places of decimal.

(1)	86432 ÷ 197	**(2)**	343762 ÷ 1654
(3)	48436 ÷ 168	**(4)**	56336 ÷ 198
(5)	43643 ÷ 894	**(6)**	87643 ÷ 976

(7)   732162 ÷ 1898   **(8)**   17326 ÷ 978

(9)   17632 ÷ 687   **(10)**   10132 ÷ 1874

(11)   36242 ÷ 884   **(12)**   876321 ÷ 1984

Answers:

(1) 438.7411	**(2)** 207.8367	**(3)** 288.3095
(4) 284.5252	**(5)** 48.8176	**(6)** 89.7981
(7) 385.7544	**(8)** 17.7157	**(9)** 25.6652
(10) 5.4066	**(11)** 40.9977	**(12)** 441.694

SQUARES

Squares of a number ending with 5

Although I have explained this earlier in the chapter on First Formula, I shall explain it again for the benefit of the students.

$$
\begin{array}{r}
85^2 \quad = \quad 85 \\
\times\ 85 \\
\hline
7225 \\
\hline
\end{array}
$$

Steps:

- Multiply 5 by 5 and put composite digit 25 on the right-hand side.
- Add 1 to the upper left-hand digit 8 i.e. 8 +1 = 9.
- Multiply 9 to the lower left-hand digit 8, i.e. $9 \times 8 = 72$, put this on the left-hand side.
- Our answer is 7225.

Using this method, we can find out the square of any two-digit number ending with 5.

Problems:

(1) $(15)^2$ (2) $(25)^2$ (3) $(35)^2$ (4) $(45)^2$

(5) $(55)^2$ (6) $(65)^2$ (7) $(75)^2$ (8) $(85)^2$

(9) $(95)^2$ **(10)** $(105)^2$ **(11)** $(115)^2$ **(12)** $(125)^2$

(13) $(135)^2$ **(14)** $(145)^2$ **(15)** $(155)^2$ **(16)** $(165)^2$

Answers:

(1) 225	**(2)** 625	**(3)** 1225	**(4)** 2025
(5) 3025	**(6)** 4225	**(7)** 5625	**(8)** 7225
(9) 9025	**(10)** 11025	**(11)** 13225	**(12)** 15625
(13) 18225	**(14)** 21025	**(15)** 24025	**(16)** 27225

Finding squares of an adjacent number

Forward method:

If we know the square of a number, say ($75^2 = 5625$), how do we find out the square of 76.

$$75^2 = 5625 \text{ (known)}$$
$$76^2 = 75^2 + (75 + 76) = 5625 = 5776$$
$$\begin{array}{r} 5625 \\ + 151 \\ \hline 5776 \end{array}$$

Steps:

It is very easy. The format shown above is self explanatory. But I am explaining it for the benefit of the students:

- 75^2 = 5625 is known
- Add (75 + 76 = 151) to this to get 76^2
- 76^2 = 5776.

Problems:

(1) $(36)^2$	**(2)** $(37)^2$	**(3)** $(46)^2$	**(4)** $(56)^2$
(5) $(57)^2$	**(6)** $(66)^2$	**(7)** $(67)^2$	**(8)** $(86)^2$
(9) $(96)^2$	**(10)** $(97)^2$		

Answers:

(1) 1296	**(2)** 1369	**(3)** 2116	**(4)** 3136
(5) 3249	**(6)** 4356	**(7)** 4489	**(8)** 7396
(9) 9216	**(10)** 9409		

Reverse method

Did you like the forward method? You have learnt to find out the square of a number which is 1 more than the given number whose square is known.

Now let me explain the reverse method through which you will be able to find out squares of a number which is one less than the given number.

Let me explain with an example:

Suppose we know the square of a number, say 70; how do we find out the square of 69?

$(70)^2$ = 4900 (known)

$(69)^2$ = $4900 - (69 + 70) = 4900 - 139 = 4761$

Problems:

(1) $(29)^2$	**(2)** $(24)^2$	**(3)** $(34)^2$	**(4)** $(39)^2$
(5) $(44)^2$	**(6)** $(49)^2$	**(7)** $(54)^2$	**(8)** $(59)^2$
(9) $(64)^2$	**(10)** $(69)^2$	**(11)** $(74)^2$	**(12)** $(79)^2$
(13) $(84)^2$	**(14)** $(89)^2$	**(15)** $(94)^2$	**(16)** $(99)^2$

Answers:

(1) 841	**(2)** 576	**(3)** 1156	**(4)** 1521
(5) 1936	**(6)** 2401	**(7)** 2916	**(8)** 3481
(9) 4096	**(10)** 4761	**(11)** 5476	**(12)** 6241
(13) 7056	**(14)** 7921	**(15)** 8836	**(16)** 9801

Mental formula for finding squares.

Let us first find the square of 11 using the formula:

$$11^2 = 11 + 1 / 1^2 = 12/1 = 121$$

The formula is self explanatory. However, let me explain it for more clarification:

- The slash used here is just a separator.
- Our operating zone is 10×1 or simply 10.
- 11 is one more than 10.
- We added 1 to 11 to make it 12.
- The number of digits after the slash can be only one.
- If the number of digits after the slash exceeds one, then we place only the rightmost digit on the extreme right after the slash, and the remaining digits get added to the number on the left-hand side of the slash.

Will you be able to find the squares of other numbers in a similar manner ? Try.....

$12^2 = 12 + 2 / 2^2$ $\qquad\qquad = 14/4 = 144$

$13^2 = 13 + 3 / 3^2$ $\qquad\qquad = 16/9 = 169$

$14^2 = 14 + 4 / 4^2$ $\qquad\qquad = 18/16$
(Apply step no. 6 here) $18 / {}_16 = 196$

$15^2 = 15 + 5 / 5^2$ $\qquad\qquad = 20/25$
(Apply step no. 6 here)
$\qquad\qquad\qquad 20 / {}_25 = 225$

$16^2 = 16 + 6 / 6^2$ $\qquad = 22 / {}_36 = 256$

You can work like this up to 19^2. What about the numbers above 20?

The formula remains the same with a slight change.

21^2 = $2 \times (21 + 1) / 1^2 = 2 \times (22) / 1 = 44/1 = 441$

This change is because now we are operating in the 10×2 zone. Is it going to hold good for the whole range from 21 to 29? Let us check:

$22^2 = 2 \times (22 + 2) / 2^2$ = $2 \times (24) / 4 = 48/4 = 484$

$23^2 = 2 \times (23 + 3) / 3^2$ = $2 \times (26) / 9 = 52/9 = 529$

$24^2 = 2 \times (24 + 4) / 4^2$ = $2 \times (28) / 16 = 56/_16 = 576$

Having learnt this, can you now find out the squares of the numbers 31 to 39?

$31^2 = 3 \times (31 + 1) / 1^2$ = $3 \times (32) / 1 = 96 / 1 = 961$

By the method explained above, you should be able to easily memorise the squares of numbers up to 99 without much hassle.

CUBES

To find out cubes of a two-digit number, we take the help of the formula:

$$(a + b)^3 = a^3 + 3a^2b + 3ab^2 + b^3$$

This can be written as:

$$a^3 + a^2b + ab^2 + b^3$$
$$2a^2b \qquad 2ab^2$$
$$\overline{}$$

We have simply broken $3a^2b$ and $3ab^2$ into two parts a^2b and a^2b and ab^2 and $2ab^2$, to simplify the matter.

In the above formula, we see that the terms a^3, a^2b, ab^2, and b^3 are placed at the top and the two terms $2a^2b$ and $2ab^2$ are placed at the bottom. The complete formula comes into being when you add the terms at the top to those at the bottom.

If we scrutinise the top term closely, then we find that:

$a^3 \times b/a = a^2b; a^2b \times b/a = ab^2$ and $ab^2 \times b/a = b^3$

The common ratio between the top terms is b/a. This is the ultimate finding.

We have to only dig out b/a and our desired result will be there.

Let me explain this with the help of an example:

1 2^3,   We have a = 1, a^3 = 1, b = 2 and b/a = 2
a b

Steps:

- Our first term is a^3 = (1) ^{3} = 1.
- The second term is a^2 b = (a)^3 × b/a = 1×2 = 2.
- The third term is ab^2 = (a^2 b) × b/a = 2 × 2 = 4.
- The fourth term is b^3 = (a b^2) × b/a = 4 × 2 = 8.
- Put all this in the first row, maintaining a space.
- For the second row, double the two middle terms i.e. a^2 b = 2 so that 2 a^2 b = 4 and ab^2 = 4 so 2ab^2 = 8. Second row comes as 4 and 8.
- Now add them.

```
    1  2  4  8
       4  8
    _____
    1  7  2  8  -  Answer
       1        -  Remainder at each stage
```

Let us find 16^3; here a = 1, b = 6 and $\frac{b}{a}$ = 6, a^3 = 1

```
16³   =1  6  36  216
          12 72
      _____
       4  0   9   6  - Answer
       3  12  21      - Remainder at each stage
```

Steps explained:

- From the digit in the right 216, the unit digit 6 is retained as part of the answer and the remainder 21 is added to the left.

- After adding the remainder 21 to (36 + 72) we get 129. 9 is retained as the answer and 12 is added to the left.

- On adding the remainder 12 to the left we get 30. 0 is retained and 3 is added to the left.

- Adding the digits on the extreme left gives 4. The answer is 4096. Our operation is over now.

Let us take another example to clarify our method further:

- 21^3 Here, a = 2, b = 1, a^3 = 8 and $\frac{b}{a} = \frac{1}{2}$

$$21^3 \quad = 8 \quad 4 \quad 2 \quad 1$$
$$ 8 \quad 4$$
$$\overline{9 \quad 2 \quad 6 \quad 1}$$
$$\cancel{1}$$

- 22^3 Here, a = 2, b = 2a^3 = 8 and $\frac{b}{a}$ = 1

$$22^3 \quad = 8 \quad 8 \quad 8 \quad 8$$
$$ 16 \quad 16$$
$$\overline{10 \quad 6 \quad 4 \quad 8}$$
$$\cancel{2}\ \cancel{2}$$

- 25^3 Here, a = 2, a^3 = 8, b = 5 and $\frac{b}{a} = \frac{5}{2}$

$$25^3 \quad = 8 \quad 20 \quad 50 \quad 125$$
$$ 40 \quad 100$$
$$\overline{15 \quad 6 \quad 2 \quad 5}\ \text{- Answer}$$
$$\cancel{7}\ \cancel{16}\ \cancel{12}\ \text{- Remainder at each stage}$$

- 27^3 Here, $a = 2$, $a^3 = 8$, $b = 7$ and $\frac{b}{a} = \frac{7}{2}$

$$27^3 = 8 \quad 28 \quad 98 \quad 343$$
$$56 \quad 196$$

| 19 6 | 8 | 3 | - Answer |

~~11 32 34~~ - Remainder at each stage

In this way you can find cubes of any two-digit numbers.

Problems:

(1) 14^3	**(2)** 17^3	**(3)** 18^3
(4) 19^3	**(5)** 24^3	**(6)** 26^3
(7) 28^3	**(8)** 29^3	**(9)** 31^3
(10) 32^3	**(11)** 33^3	**(12)** 37^3
(13) 39^3	**(14)** 42^3	**(15)** 46^3
(16) 45^3	**(17)** 47^3	**(18)** 48^3
(19) 49^3	**(20)** 52^3	**(21)** 53^3
(22) 54^3	**(23)** 55^3	**(24)** 56^3
(25) 57^3	**(26)** 58^3	**(27)** 59^3
(28) 61^3	**(29)** 62^3	**(30)** 63^3

Answers:

(1) 2744	**(2)** 4913	**(3)** 5832
(4) 6859	**(5)** 13824	**(6)** 17576
(7) 21952	**(8)** 24389	**(9)** 29791

(10) 32768	**(11)** 35937	**(12)** 50653
(13) 59319	**(14)** 74088	**(15)** 97336
(16) 91125	**(17)** 103823	**(18)** 110592
(19) 117649	**(20)** 140608	**(21)** 148877
(22) 157464	**(23)** 166375	**(24)** 175616
(25) 185193	**(26)** 195112	**(27)** 205379
(28) 226981	**(29)** 238328	**(30)** 250047

SQUARE ROOTS

Square root of a perfect square

For finding square roots, we are required to have some background. Let us see:

			Last digit
1^2	=	1	1
2^2	=	4	4
3^2	=	9	9
4^2	=	16	6
5^2	=	25	5
6^2	=	36	6
7^2	=	49	9
8^2	=	64	4
9^2	=	81	1
10^2	=	100	00

After reading the example given, we can say that perfect squares end with 1, 4, 5, 6, 9 and 00, or that a perfect square does not end with 2, 3, 7 and 8.

Also,

The number of digits in a square root will

be $\frac{n}{2}$ or $\frac{(n+1)}{2}$

And,

We have to learn to find the 'Duplex' of a number.

Number	Duplex
a	a^2
ab	2 ab
abc	2 [ac] + b^2
abcd	2 ad + 2 bc
abcde	2 ae + 2 bd + c^2
abcdef	2 af + 2 be + 2 cd

Number	Duplex
2	$2^2 = 4$
21	$2 \times (2 \times 1) = 4$
212	$2 \times (2 \times 2) + 1^2 = 9$
2124	$2 (2 \times 4) + 2 (1 \times 2) = 20$
21243	$2 (2 \times 3) + (1 \times 4) + 2^2 = 24$

Knowledge of the duplex is required to find out square roots.

Let me explain with the help of an example:

$$\sqrt{2116}$$

	2	1	:	1	6
8			5		3
	4	6	:	0	

Steps:

- Group the numbers as per the pairing technique known to you. (Start from the last digit and make a group taking two digits together).

- Find out the first answer digit by the method known to you. In the above example, the first answer digit is 4.

- Put 4 in the answer place (See the division format for the answer place) and keep the double of the first answer digit i.e. $2 \times 4 = 8$ as the divisor.

Now we are ready to find the square root.

	21		16
8		5	3
	46		

- Here our gross dividend is 51; 8 goes 6 times and the remainder is 3.

  Our problem is solved. We have found the square root to be 46 (n/2 =4/2 = 2), but let me explain it further.

- Our next gross dividend is 36, from which we will subtract the duplex of 6, i.e. $6^2 = 36$.

	2	1		1		6
8			5		3	
		46		0		

- We get the remainder as 0.

Salient points explained:

- Like division, finding the square root is also a two-step process — Division + Direction.

  Here our divisor becomes double the first answer digit, and by way of direction, we subtract the duplex of the quotient numbers, leaving only the first answer digit.

104

- We keep the first answer digit separate while finding out the duplex.

Now let me take an example to clarify:

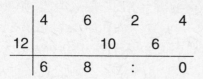

```
    4    6    2    4
12           10    6
  ─────────────────────
    6    8    :    0
```

Steps:

- We found the first answer digit to be 6. The divisor becomes 12.

- 46-36=10 (remainder) is written before the next digit 2.

- The gross dividend is 102; 12 goes 8 times and the remainder is equal to 6. 6 is put before 4 as shown.

- Now our gross dividend is 64. As part of direction, we subtract $8^2 = 64$ from this and obtain 0.

Note:

You can avoid the last step if you wish to, as from our previous knowledge we know that the digits in, the square root will be n/2 = 2, and the example taken above is a complete square.

```
    1    2    9    9    6
2   0    0    0
  ─────────────────────
    1    1    4    :    0
```

Steps:

- We found the first answer digit to be 1. Divisor becomes 2.

105

- 1 -1 = 0 is written before the next digit 2.
- Our next gross dividend is 2; 2 goes 1 time and R = 0.
- Direction — next gross dividend = 9. As part of the direction, we subtract $1^2 = 1$ from 9 and obtain 8.
- Divide 8 by 2 – 2 goes 4 times and R = 0. Our operation is complete here as we have already got a three-digit answer = $\frac{(n+1)}{2}$. We will now proceed to find the remainder.
- Direction — Next gross dividend 09.

$$
\begin{array}{c|ccccc}
 & 1 & 2 & 9 & 9 & 6 \\
12 & 0 & 0 & 0 & & \\
\hline
 & 1 & 1 & 4 & &
\end{array}
$$

Direction Step 1   = 09 - Duplex of 14
                    09 - 2 × (1 × 4) = 1

Direction Step 2   = 16 - Duplex of 4
                    $16 - 4^2 = 0$

So the remainder = 0

Example:

$\sqrt{125316}$

$$
\begin{array}{c|cccccc}
 & 1 & 2 & 5 & 3 & 1 & 6 \\
6 & & & 3 & 5 & 4 & \\
\hline
 & 3 & 5 & 4 & : & &
\end{array}
$$

(1)
$$
\begin{array}{r}
53 \\
- 25 \\
\hline
28
\end{array}
$$

(2)
$$
\begin{array}{r}
41 \\
- 40 \\
\hline
16 \\
16 \\
\hline
00
\end{array}
$$

Steps explained in short:

- First answer, digit 3, R = 3, Divisor = 6.
- Gross dividend, 35. Divide by 6, Q = 5, R = 5.
- Gross dividend, 53, take direction and subtract the duplex of 5 from 53. It comes to 28. Divide by 6,

  Q = 4, R = 4. The operation is complete here.

Take Direction

- 41 - Duplex of 54 = 41 − 2 (20) = 1.
  (6 will be put down on 1 to make it 16)

- 16 - Duplex of 4 = 16-16 = 0. [Remainder = 0]

Finding the square root in decimals

In all the above examples I have found remainders but let us try to find square roots of incomplete squares.

Example:

$$\sqrt{73\,21\,08}$$

	73	2	1	0	8		(1)	121
16		9	12	16	14	15		− 25
	8	5 5	6	3 3				96

Step explained:

Number of digits in square root = $\frac{n}{2}$ = 3

- First answer digit 8, R = 9, Divisor = 16
- 92 ÷ 16, Q = 5, R = 12
- 121 - Duplex of 5 = 96
- 96 ÷ 16, Q = 5, R = 16
  {If we take Q = 6, then negative comes}

(1)
121
− 25
—
96

(2)
160
− 50
—
110

(3)
148
− 85
—
63

(4)
150
− 90
—
60

We have found three required answer digits before the decimal. Now we will proceed towards finding the answer digit after the decimal.

- 160 − Duplex of 55 = 110
- 110 ÷ 16, Q = 6, R = 14
- 148 − Duplex of 556 [$2 \times (5 \times 6) + 5^2$]
    =148-85=63
- 63 ÷ 16, Q = 3, R = 15

- Add 00 in the dividend and take 150 as the gross dividend, 150 − Duplex of 5563 = 150 $[2 \times (5 \times 3) + 2 \times (5 \times 6)]$
- $60 \div 16$, Q = 3, R = 12
- Our answer is 855.633

Problems:

(1) 186241	**(2)** 225646	**(3)** 38123
(4) 25362	**(5)** 1681	**(6)** 2025
(7) 18634	**(8)** 199432	**(9)** 106324
(10) 10876	**(11)** 13637	**(12)** 98436
(13) 63473	**(14)** 742822	**(15)** 898426
(16) 60123	**(17)** 163462	**(18)** 131261
(19) 50217	**(20)** 48324	

Answers:

(1) 431.566	**(2)** 475.022	**(3)** 195.251
(4) 159.254	**(5)** 41	**(6)** 45
(7) 136.506	**(8)** 446.578	**(9)** 326.073
(10) 104.288	**(11)** 116.777	**(12)** 313.745
(13) 251.938	**(14)** 861.871	**(15)** 947.853
(16) 245.199	**(17)** 404.304	**(18)** 362.299
(19) 224.091	**(20)** 219.827	

Cube Roots

Finding cube roots requires some background.

			Last digit
1^3	=	1	1
2^3	=	8	8
3^3	=	27	7
4^3	=	64	4
5^3	=	125	5
6^3	=	216	6
7^3	=	343	3
8^3	=	512	2
9^3	=	729	9

From the above illustration we can make out that the last digit of 2^3 is 8, 3^3 is 7 and vice versa. All the others repeat themselves.

Procedure of finding a cube

- Start from the right and put a comma when the three digits are over.

Example:

     — 9,261

     — 1,728

     — 32,768

     — 175,616

- After putting the comma, see the last digit of the number, compare that with the table provided above. You will get the last digit.
- Now see the first group of numbers and ascertain which number's cube is less than the group. That number is your first digit.
- You have thus found the first digit and the last digit.

Let us take an example:

*   9, 261

    2   1

Steps:

- Counting from the last, we put a comma after 9.
- By seeing the last digit, we ascertain that the last digit of the cube root will be 1.
- Now we see 9 and ascertain that $2^3 = 8$ is less than 9 and $3^3 = 27$ is more.
- Our first digit thus comes to 2, and the answer is 21.

Another example:

    32, 768

     3   2

- We find the cube root of the last digit which is equa' to 2.

- For the first two digits - 32, we put 3 as our first digit as $3^3 = 27$ is less than 3^2 and $4^3 = 64$ is more.
- Our answer is 32.

Note:

This technique is valid for exact cubes only.

This is a good method of finding approximations.

Simultaneous Equations

Simultaneous equation is a topic which comes in use frequently. Therefore I have decided to cover this topic in the book.

Let me start with an example:

$$5x \quad - \quad 3y \quad = \quad 11$$
$$6x \quad - \quad 5y \quad = \quad 9$$

If in this example we are able to find the value of x, then finding the value of y is not very difficult. To find the value of x we make an operational point.

* Operational point

$$x = \frac{\text{Numerator}}{\text{Denominator}}$$

Numerator

(Coefficient of y in the 1st row × constant in the 2nd row) - Coefficient of y in the 2nd row × constant in the 1st row) [Coefficients are taken with the signs intact]

Thus the numerator (N) = $(-3 \times 9) - (-5 \times 11)$
$$= -27 + 55 = 28$$

For denominator:

* Operational point

$$5x \searrow - \nearrow 3y = 11$$
$$6x \nearrow - \searrow 5y = 9$$

Denominator

(Coefficient of y in the 1st row × coefficient of x in the 2nd row) – (Coefficient of y in the 2nd row × coefficient of x in 1st row) [Coefficients are taken with the signs intact]

The denominator $= (-3 \times 6) - (-5 \times 5)$
$$= -18 + 25 = 7$$

$$x = \frac{\text{Numerator}}{\text{Denominator}}$$

$$= \frac{28}{7} = 4$$

Problems:

- $11x \times 6y = 28$
  $7x - 4y = 10$

- $3x + 2y = 4$
  $8x + 5y = 9$

- $2x + 3y = 12$
  $3x - 2y = 5$

- $7x + 9y = 85$
  $4x + 5y = 48$

Answers:

(1) $x = 2, y = 1$ **(2)** $x = -2, y = 5$

(3) $x = 3, y = 2$ **(4)** $x = 7, y = 4$

Peculiar Types

Type - 1

Example:

$$6x + 7y = 8$$
$$19x + 14y = 16$$

Solve it for x and y.

How much time would you take to solve it? A couple of minutes.

In this case, are you able to see that the coefficients of y and the constants are in the same ratio.

i.e. $\dfrac{7}{14} = \dfrac{8}{16}$

The formula says, that when one is in ratio then the other is 0. In this equation you find that the coefficient of y is in ratio with the constant term, therefore $x = 0$.

Answer: $x = 0$ and

$$y = +\ \frac{8}{7}$$

Check it yourself:

$$12x + 78y = 12 \quad \text{Answer} : y = 0,\ x = 1$$
$$16x + 96y = 16$$

Type - II

$$45x - 23y = 113$$
$$23x - 45y = 91$$

115

Whenever you find x and y coefficients interchanged, then add it once and subtract it once. This reduces the large coefficients into workable coefficients. Let us see how:

Addition gives us:

$$68x - 68y = 204$$
$$68 (x - y) = 204$$
$$\text{or } x - y = 3$$

Subtraction gives us:

Answer:

$$x = 2, \quad y = -1$$
$$22x + 22y = 22$$
$$22 (x + y) = 22$$
$$\text{or } x + y = 1$$

After this, finding x and y becomes easy.

Find it yourself:

(1) $37x + 219y = 92$
$29x + 37y = 103$

(2) $12x + 17y = 53$
$17x + 12y = 63$

Answers:

(1) $x = 1, y = 2$ **(2)** $x = 3, y = 1$

A Word To All Maths Enthusiasts

My dear friends,

Every one I met praised 'Vedic Mathematics'. Many people had other books on Vedic mathematics with them but were not using them. This, I found, was due to a lot of unexplained steps.

In my book, I have tried to explain the intermediate steps in detail. If you are able to understand the "Magical Methods", then recommend this book to your friends.

The price of this book has been kept low so that these methods which have been drawn from our ancient knowledge bank "Vedas" should spread with lightening speed.

I welcome your suggestions for the improvement of this book. Win prizes for the best suggestions.

PRADEEP KUMAR
B.Tech, MBA – IIM Bangalore

The 'Achiever' Institute

Achiever is an organisation founded by Mr. Pradeep Kumar - an IIM alumni - in July 1998 to cater to the students of Gurgaon, in India. There was a lack of training institutes in Gurgaon that specifically trained, students for the MBA/ CAT entrance examinations. Mr. Kumar was quite aware of this, and so he took up the initiative to start Achiever.

The CAT examination is known for its surprise elements, which calls for a balanced approach. In this examination, two things are of prime importance (1) Ability to calculate fast and (2) Ability to read fast.

Achiever's training is based on these two crucial elements. Apart from the syllabi, Achiever teaches the students "Magical Methods of Fast Calculations". These magical methods are 10 to 15 times faster than the conventional methods. Also, Achiever has developed exercises to increase the reading speed of a person from a nominal speed to 800-1000 words per minute.

Now Achiever offers the following:
- Classroom training for MBA/CAT aspirants
- A Foundation Course for MBA/CAT aspirants (Postal-for students in their 2nd year of Graduation)
- GD and Interview Preparation for MBA/CAT aspirants

- Sharpen Your Saw - Workshop on Magical Methods of Fast Calculations and Reading Speed Enhancement
- Magical Methods of Fast Calculations - for Schools (Class 9 and above)
- Mock Interviews (for candidates going to face job interviews).